Fresh Ways
with Salads

Time-Life Books Inc.
is a wholly owned subsidiary of
TIME INCORPORATED

FOUNDER: Henry R. Luce 1898-1967

Editor-in-Chief: Henry Anatole Grunwald
President: J. Richard Munro
Chairman of the Board: Ralph P. Davidson
Corporate Editor: Ray Cave
Group Vice President, Books: Reginald K. Brack Jr.
Vice President, Books: George Artandi

COVER
Shredded beef cooked with hoisin sauce, then chilled, is set off colorfully by vinegar-marinated carrot strips and the crisp leaves of Nappa cabbage (recipe, page 124).

TIME-LIFE BOOKS INC.

EDITOR: George Constable
Director of Design: Louis Klein
Director of Editorial Resources: Phyllis K. Wise
Acting Text Director: Ellen Phillips
Editorial Board: Russell B. Adams Jr., Dale M. Brown, Roberta Conlan, Thomas H. Flaherty, Donia Ann Steele, Rosalind Stubenberg, Kit van Tulleken, Henry Woodhead
Director of Photography and Research:
John Conrad Weiser

PRESIDENT: Reginald K. Brack Jr.
Executive Vice Presidents: John M. Fahey Jr., Christopher T. Linen
Senior Vice Presidents: James L. Mercer, Leopoldo Toralballa
Vice Presidents: Stephen L. Bair, Ralph J. Cuomo, Neal Goff, Stephen L. Goldstein, Juanita T. James, Hallett Johnson III, Robert H. Smith, Paul R. Stewart
Director of Production Services: Robert J. Passantino

Editorial Operations
Copy Chief: Diane Ullius
Editorial Operations: Caroline A. Boubin (manager)
Production: Celia Beattie
Quality Control: James J. Cox (director)
Library: Louise D. Forstall

Correspondents: Elisabeth Kraemer-Singh (Bonn); Maria Vincenza Aloisi (Paris); Ann Natanson (Rome).

Library of Congress Cataloguing in Publication Data
Main entry under title:
Fresh ways with salads.
  (Healthy home cooking)
  Includes index.
  1. Salads. I. Time-Life Books. II. Series.
TX740.F66 1986   641.8'3   86-14351
ISBN 0-8094-5824-1
ISBN 0-8094-5825-X (lib. bdg.)

For information on and a full description of any of the Time-Life Books series listed above, please call 1-800-621-7026 or write:
Reader Information
Time-Life Customer Service
P.O. Box C-32068
Richmond, Virginia 23261-2068

HEALTHY HOME COOKING

SERIES DIRECTOR: Dale M. Brown
Deputy Editor: Barbara Fleming
Series Administrator: Elise Ritter Gibson
Designer: Herbert H. Quarmby
Picture Editor: Sally Collins
Photographer: Renée Comet
Text Editor: Allan Fallow
Editorial Assistant: Rebecca C. Christoffersen

Editorial Staff for *Fresh Ways with Salads:*
Book Manager: Andrea E. Reynolds
Assistant Picture Editor: Scarlet Cheng
Researcher/Writer: Susan Stuck
Writer: Margery A. duMond
Copy Coordinators: Elizabeth Graham, Ruth Baja Williams
Picture Coordinator: Linda Yates
Photographer's Assistant: Rina M. Ganassa

Special Contributors: Mary Jane Blandford (food purchasing), Robert J. Chambers and Lisa Cherkasky (recipe development and styling), Carol Gvozdich (nutrient analysis), Nancy Lendved (props), Tajvana Queen (kitchen assistant), Bryce Walker (text), CiCi Williamson (microwave section)

THE COOKS

ADAM DE VITO began his cooking apprenticeship at L'Auberge Chez François near Washington, D.C., when he was only 14. He has worked at Washington's Le Pavillon restaurant, taught with cookbook author Madeleine Kamman, and conducted classes at L'Académie de Cuisine in Maryland.

HENRY GROSSI, who started his cooking career with a New York caterer, earned a Grand Diplôme at the École de Cuisine La Varenne in Paris. He then served as the school's assistant director and as its North American business and publications coordinator.

JOHN T. SHAFFER is a graduate of The Culinary Institute of America at Hyde Park, New York. He has had broad experience as a chef, including five years at The Four Seasons Hotel in Washington, D.C., where he was *chef saucier* at Aux Beaux Champs restaurant.

THE CONSULTANT

CAROL CUTLER is the prizewinning author of many cookbooks, including *The Six-Minute Soufflé and Other Culinary Delights* and *Pâté: The New Main Course for the 80's;* she also writes about food and entertaining for national magazines and newspapers. During the 12 years she lived in France, she studied at the Cordon Bleu and the École des Trois Gourmandes, as well as with private chefs. She is a member of the Cercle des Gourmettes, as well as a charter member and past president of Les Dames D'Escoffier.

THE NUTRITION CONSULTANT

JANET TENNEY has been involved in nutrition and consumer affairs since she received her master's degree in human nutrition from Columbia University. She is the manager for developing and implementing nutritional programs for a major chain of supermarkets in the Washington, D.C., area.

SPECIAL CONSULTANT

SANDRA CONRAD STRAUSS, the former vice president of consumer affairs for the United Fresh Fruit and Vegetable Association, is president of Consumer Concepts, Oakton, Virginia, a consulting firm specializing in consumer education about fresh produce. She is the author of *Fancy Fruits and Extraordinary Vegetables,* a cookbook that features some of the more unfamiliar and unusual produce items available in supermarkets today.

Nutritional analyses for *Fresh Ways with Salads* were derived from Practorcare's Nutriplanner System and other current data.

Other Publications:

AMERICAN COUNTRY
VOYAGE THROUGH THE UNIVERSE
THE THIRD REICH
THE TIME-LIFE GARDENER'S GUIDE
MYSTERIES OF THE UNKNOWN
TIME FRAME
FIX IT YOURSELF
FITNESS, HEALTH & NUTRITION
SUCCESSFUL PARENTING
UNDERSTANDING COMPUTERS
LIBRARY OF NATIONS
THE ENCHANTED WORLD
THE KODAK LIBRARY OF CREATIVE PHOTOGRAPHY
GREAT MEALS IN MINUTES
THE CIVIL WAR
PLANET EARTH
COLLECTOR'S LIBRARY OF THE CIVIL WAR
THE EPIC OF FLIGHT
THE GOOD COOK
WORLD WAR II
HOME REPAIR AND IMPROVEMENT
THE OLD WEST

This volume is one of a series of illustrated cookbooks that emphasize the preparation of healthful dishes for today's weight-conscious, nutrition-minded eaters.

Fresh Ways
with Salads

BY

THE EDITORS OF TIME-LIFE BOOKS

TIME-LIFE BOOKS / ALEXANDRIA, VIRGINIA

Contents

Alfalfa Sprouts and Red-Onion Salad

Midsummer Melon Salad with Almond Oil

Lobster Salad with Sweet Peppers and Cilantro

Salad's Special Magic

What fresher, more inviting food is there than salad? It seems to radiate good health, and so it should: The tenderest of greens, the crunchiest of roots, the leanest of meats and poultry, the most wholesome of grains, beans and pasta are among its raw materials. And as if this in itself were not advertisement enough of salad's virtues, it is a dish that need not be fussed over, and one that often can be made quickly. No wonder, then, that Americans are the world's great salad makers, consuming more than four billion pounds of lettuce each year, and that they have evolved this culinary art into their own specialty.

A salad can be the most varied of dishes. It may be as simple as a bowl of lettuce tossed with a light vinaigrette, or a more complex composition of meats and vegetables that might serve as a meal. Its elements can be raw or cooked or in combination, and it can be served chilled, at room temperature, or even warm. This book alone contains enough salads — 123 in all — to suit any ap-

Salads made with grains, dried beans or pasta are loaded with complex carbohydrates — the main source of energy for the body — and protein. Dried beans offer a particularly generous supply of fiber and protein; but for all their protein to be utilized by the body, they must be coupled with other foods that offer complementary proteins. As luck would have it, many of these are the very ingredients of successful modern salads — wheat, rice, meat and dairy products, to list a few. Thus the black bean and rice salad with red and green pepper strips on page 76 is not just a delicious meal; it is a highly nutritious one, supplying about a quarter of the body's daily protein needs.

As this book makes patently clear, salad need never be the same from one meal to the next. The salad maker today is aided greatly by the presence of once-exotic ingredients in the supermarket, including a wider variety of fresh herbs.

The range of available vinegars and salad oils has increased as well,

petite; what is more, they have been judiciously created to take into account today's need for lighter, healthier eating. For example, the cold lobster with peppers in a citrus vinaigrette on page 104 adds up to only 190 calories a serving; the asparagus salad with Jerusalem artichoke on page 21 comes to about 46 calories per portion.

Even the ancient Greeks knew that salad was healthful; they held it to be a food of the gods. In Shakespeare's England, so-called fountains of youth, assembled from the first tender herbs and lettuces of spring, were eagerly consumed as antidotes to the grim winter diet. The great French gastronome Brillat-Savarin summed it up nicely: "Salad refreshes without weakening and comforts without irritating," he wrote in 1825, "and it makes us younger."

Whether truly rejuvenating or not, salad is, with its endless choice of ingredients, a bountiful source of minerals, vitamins and other nutrients. And when it is dressed carefully, salad will be low in fat as well, and thus in calories. The fact that most lettuces are between 90 and 95 percent water is bound to give some people reason to cheer.

along with the number of prepared mustards. Imported wine, tarragon, balsamic and Chinese-black vinegars lend a new liveliness to salad dressings, as do oils as diverse as walnut, almond and dark sesame.

Freshness above all

America's salad bounty is enhanced still further by the seasonal appearance of several delightful ingredients. Asparagus might well stand as the emblem of spring; tomatoes plump and red from basking in the sun evoke summer, as does golden corn, its kernels swollen with sweet juice. Cabbages and root vegetables show up abundantly in fall. Many of the recipes in this volume would greatly benefit from the inclusion of vegetables picked at their peak of ripeness and flavor. The rise of farmers' markets in many cities has made this possible by putting an array of perfectly ripened ingredients at the salad maker's disposal.

Fruit has played a time-honored role in many salads. A greater availability of seasonal produce and an increase in creativity have left the dieter's staple of yore — a canned peach half topped with a scoop of cottage cheese and served on a bed of tasteless iceberg lettuce — happily outmoded. New marriages of fruit and meat, seafood or vegetables have taken place. In this book, for example, chicken is coupled with grapefruits *(page 119)*, pork with nectarines and oranges *(page 122)*, shrimp with pineapple and mangoes *(page 107)*, and kale with pears *(page 52)*, all to delicious effect.

Although the recipes call for fresh ingredients, salads of course can be a wonderful vehicle for leftovers. Providing they have not been previously buttered, cooked green beans, well chilled from their overnight stay in the refrigerator, make a lively luncheon dish when tossed with a vinaigrette. Likewise, leftover poultry and meats lend themselves to intriguing combinations with greens, fresh herbs and simple dressings.

Simplicity as a goal

With the possibilities for salads limitless, the temptation often has been to put in too much. One recipe from the 17th century calls for almonds, raisins, figs, spinach, olives, capers, currants, sage, cucumbers, red cabbage, orange and lemon. Our cooks have been more selective, balancing flavors and bearing in mind a particular salad's place in the meal as first course, main course or side dish. They have mixed complementary greens and paired foods and seasonings that share a natural affinity, such as tomatoes and basil, rice and saffron, cucumber and dill. At the same time, the cooks have sought contrasts in texture, combining, for instance, dried apricots, wild rice and water chestnuts *(page 70)*, or crab with spinach and corn *(page 110)*. They have also taken color into account, and perhaps there are no more compelling examples than the oven-roasted vegetable salad with shrimp and scallops on page 108, or the corn salad on page 17 with its strips of red and green peppers and bits of red onion.

The recipes have been designed to encourage imaginative, well-balanced eating. Serving portions are based on the following measures: ½ to ¾ of a cup when a salad is to be eaten as a side dish or a first course, 1 to 1¼ cups for a main course at lunch, and 1½ to 2½ cups for one that is to be consumed as a main course at dinner. For salads with cooked ingredients, use the smaller portion size in all instances. If you wish to serve larger portions, which means more calories, take into account the rest of the day's eating in your menu planning and compensate for the increased calories by selecting appropriate foods.

The first section of the book explores some unusual combinations of greens, vegetables and fruits. The second delves into grains, dried beans and pasta, while the third serves up salads based on meats, poultry and seafood. In the final section, the microwave oven offers shortcuts to salad making. A gallery of the herbs used in the recipes appears on pages 138 and 139.

A glossary describes uncommon ingredients and cooking terms.

Whatever the components of a salad, it is the dressing that ties them together. In this book, each dressing has been created with an eye to limiting the fat and calories, generally through a reduction in the amount of oil used. Still, even reduced-oil dressings must contain calories. Thus anyone seriously concerned about lowering caloric intake should use a dressing sparingly, pouring on just enough to moisten and flavor the salad.

Handling salad ingredients

The success of a salad — particularly one calling for greens — depends greatly on how the ingredients are handled beforehand. If the salad is to be truly delicious, only the freshest of produce will do. Select greens that are crisp and well colored. (The darker the lettuces, the more vitamin A they will contain.)

The greens should be washed under cold running water. With head lettuce, pluck away the leaves and pay particular attention to their bases, where soil may cling. Discard any leaves that are wilted, have frayed edges or are blemished. Grit-prone greens — spinach, for example — will come clean when gently swirled several times in a bowl of water. Once they have been washed, the greens should be removed from the water, drained and then carefully dried — either by patting them between paper towels or by whirling them in a salad spinner. The removal of clinging water ensures that the dressing will coat the salad evenly and that the leaves will remain crisp.

If the washed greens are not to be used immediately, they may be stored for a day in the refrigerator, in a plastic bag, with a paper towel wrapped around them to soak up any excess moisture. Fresh herbs also benefit from respectful treatment; packed loosely in a closed container, they will remain vigorous a week or more in the refrigerator. Some cooks trim the stems, particularly of herbs that come in bunches, then stand the herbs in a glass or jar filled with water and keep them in the refrigerator lightly covered with plastic wrap.

For a natural-looking salad, tear the lettuce leaves by hand into pieces of the size you want — unless, of course, the recipe specifies otherwise. To preserve crispness, do this shortly before the salad is to be served and be sure to apply the dressing at the very last minute. Then toss or otherwise mix the salad.

Perhaps the wisest words about salad preparation are some that date back three centuries. "Every plant should bear its part without being overpowered by some herb of stronger taste, so as to endanger the native savor and vertue of the rest," wrote English diarist John Evelyn in 1699. When this is accomplished, all the ingredients should "fall into their places like notes in music." Thus carefully orchestrated, the salad will win applause as one of the liveliest, most satisfying and healthiest parts of the meal.

The Burgeoning of the Greens

Salad making has benefited immeasurably from the increasing availability of hitherto esoteric or hard-to-find greens. The most popular of these are shown here and on the next three pages, with accompanying descriptions of their virtues. Among them are two vegetables, kale and mustard greens, that take on new life when eaten raw in salads.

Curly endive (chicory). This resembles Belgian endive in flavor. Although the lighter leaves are sweeter and more tender than the dark green ones, they still boast the tangy bite that is associated with all chicories.

Beet greens. Use only the freshest, youngest greens, discarding the red stems. The leaves have a flavor that resembles both spinach and beets.

Arugula (rocket). An Italian green, arugula has a pungent, slightly peppery flavor. Look for small, narrow leaves — signs of a young, sweet plant.

Belgian endive. Sharp in flavor and crisp in texture, the finest Belgian endive has tightly wrapped leaves that range in color from white to pale yellow.

The Burgeoning of the Greens

Mustard greens. With their pungent flavor, young mustard greens marry well with less assertive salad greens. Avoid the older, tougher leaves.

Nappa cabbage (Chinese cabbage). This elongated cabbage has long, broad ribs and crinkled, white to light green leaves. Select unblemished heads with firm leaves.

Oakleaf lettuce. Among the most delicate of lettuces, oakleaf does not travel well; in areas where it is grown, however, it is well worth the purchase.

Dandelion greens. Part of the chicory family, dandelion greens should be eaten before the flower appears. Farm-produced greens are milder and less tough than the wild variety.

Kale. A relative newcomer to the salad bowl, kale is an excellent source of vitamin C. Only the youngest leaves should be used, and many cooks prefer to shred them — they can be tough.

Escarole. This broad-leaved relative of curly endive shares its cousin's pleasingly bitter flavor. It is best used in combination with sweeter greens.

Mâche (corn salad, lamb's lettuce). Chewy but not crisp, this delicate green has a nutlike sweetness, with an underlying astringency. It complements dressings made with nut oils.

Basic Dressings with a New Twist

The low-fat, low-calorie dressings that follow were specially developed for this book. Several recipes call for them specifically, but the dressings can also be refrigerated for later use on salads of your own invention.

The vinaigrette suits fresh mixed greens of delicate flavor. The yogurt and buttermilk dressings marry well with assertive vegetables; they also complement meats, grains and pasta. The mayonnaise makes an ideal partner for root vegetables as well as poultry and seafood.

Any of the four may be further enhanced by the addition of herbs, spices or other seasonings. The figures found alongside each recipe give the nutrient analysis for one tablespoon of dressing.

New Mayonnaise

THIS TOFU-BASED MAYONNAISE CONTAINS JUST HALF THE AMOUNT OF EGG YOLKS AND OIL FOUND IN THE TRADITIONAL VERSION.

Makes 1½ cups

¼ lb. firm tofu, cut into small cubes and soaked in cold water for 10 minutes
½ cup plain low-fat yogurt, drained in a cheesecloth-lined colander for 10 minutes
1 egg yolk
1 tsp. dried mustard
½ cup safflower oil
¼ cup virgin olive oil
2 tbsp. white wine vinegar or cider vinegar
½ tsp. salt
½ tsp. sugar
⅛ tsp. white pepper

Calories **70**
Protein **1g.**
Cholesterol **12mg.**
Total fat **7g.**
Saturated fat **1g.**
Sodium **50mg.**

Remove the tofu from its soaking water and drain it on paper towels. Transfer the tofu to a food processor or a blender. Add the yogurt, egg yolk and mustard, and process the mixture until it is very smooth, scraping down the sides at least once.

With the motor still running, pour in the oils in a thin, steady stream, stopping halfway through the process to scrape the sides with a rubber spatula.

Add the vinegar, salt, sugar and pepper, and process the mayonnaise for 15 seconds more. Transfer the mayonnaise to a bowl and refrigerate it; the mayonnaise will keep for at least 10 days.

Vinaigrette

Makes about ½ cup

1 tsp. Dijon mustard
¼ tsp. salt
freshly ground black pepper
2½ tbsp. red wine vinegar
2½ tbsp. safflower oil
2½ tbsp. virgin olive oil

Calories **75**
Protein **0g.**
Cholesterol **0mg.**
Total fat **8g.**
Saturated fat **1g.**
Sodium **75mg.**

In a small bowl, combine the mustard, the salt, a grinding of pepper and the vinegar. Whisking vigorously, pour in the safflower oil in a thin, steady stream; incorporate the olive oil the same way. Continue whisking until the dressing is well combined. Covered and stored in the refrigerator, the dressing will keep for about a week.

Buttermilk Dressing

Makes about ½ cup

½ cup buttermilk
cayenne pepper
¼ tsp. sugar
1 shallot, finely chopped
¼ cup nonfat dry milk
2 tbsp. fresh lemon juice

Calories **15**
Protein **1g.**
Cholesterol **1mg.**
Total fat **0g.**
Saturated fat **0g.**
Sodium **30mg.**

In a small bowl, combine the buttermilk, a pinch of cayenne pepper, the sugar and the shallot. Whisk in the dry milk a tablespoon at a time, then stir in the lemon juice. To allow the dressing to thicken, cover the bowl and refrigerate it for at least 30 minutes. The dressing will keep for three days.

EDITOR'S NOTE: *The inclusion of nonfat dry milk makes for a thick, creamy dressing.*

Creamy Yogurt Dressing

Makes about ½ cup

2 tbsp. cream sherry
2 garlic cloves, finely chopped
1½ tsp. Dijon mustard
½ cup plain low-fat yogurt
1 tbsp. sour cream
⅛ tsp. white pepper

Calories **20**
Protein **1g.**
Cholesterol **2mg.**
Total fat **1g.**
Saturated fat **0g.**
Sodium **25mg.**

Put the sherry and garlic into a small saucepan. Bring the mixture to a simmer over medium heat and cook it until nearly all the liquid has evaporated — about three minutes. Transfer the mixture to a bowl. Stir in the mustard, then the yogurt, sour cream and pepper. Cover the bowl and store the dressing in the refrigerator; it will keep for two to three days.

1 *High in fiber and nutrients, the offerings of garden and orchard afford the salad maker ample room for delicious innovation.*

A Garden at the Table

Now that the opportunity for buying varied fresh ingredients has greatly increased, the cook can hardly fail to create a salad that is healthful, colorful and downright delicious every time. Still, most salad components benefit from careful handling if they are to keep all that is best about them. Certainly no one wants to sit down to a dish of limp lettuce, overcooked vegetables or discolored fruit, no matter how flavorful the dressing.

In this section, salads made predominantly with vegetables or fruit or combinations of both are featured. Such vegetables as green beans, asparagus, cauliflower, broccoli, sliced carrots, zucchini and yellow squash are often steamed, blanched or parboiled to tenderize them. Cooked this way — that is to say, briefly — all keep their crunch, and instead of losing color, an essential feature in successful salad making, most grow brighter. After being exposed to heat, the vegetables are then rinsed under cold running water to stop the cooking.

Since fruits are almost always eaten raw in a salad, they should be of juicy ripeness. Occasionally, though, a recipe will call for firm fruit; its texture and tartness can add real character to a dish. The mango and grape salad on page 60, for example, depends on the firmness of the mangoes for part of its effect.

Sliced into small pieces, with many exposed surfaces, both fruits and vegetables inevitably lose some of their nutrients. To minimize this loss, cut them up and add them to the salad as close to serving time as possible. Some fruit turns brown when it is exposed to air; use an old trick — rubbing the fruit with half a lemon or lime, or drizzling some of the juice over it — to prevent this. Not only will the fruit retain its color, but the juice will supply a little extra vitamin C and welcome bit of tartness.

Potato Salad with Peas and Sesame Seeds

Serves 8 as a side dish
Working time: about 25 minutes
Total time: about 1 hour and 15 minutes

Calories **140**
Protein **3g.**
Cholesterol **0mg.**
Total fat **6g.**
Saturated fat **1g.**
Sodium **70mg.**

1½ lb. boiling potatoes
1 lb. green peas, shelled, or 1 cup frozen peas, defrosted
3 tbsp. hulled sesame seeds
½ tsp. cumin seeds
¼ tsp. cayenne pepper
1 cucumber, peeled (if waxed) and coarsely chopped
5 scallions, trimmed and thinly sliced
3 tbsp. fresh lemon juice
¼ tsp. salt
2 tbsp. safflower oil
¼ tsp. turmeric
2 mildly hot green chili peppers, seeded, deribbed and quartered lengthwise (caution, page 17)

Boil the potatoes until they are soft when pierced with the tip of a sharp knife — 25 to 35 minutes. Remove the potatoes from the water, halve them and set them aside to cool.

Meanwhile, if you are using fresh peas, parboil them until they are tender — four to five minutes. Drain the peas and set them aside.

Heat a small, heavy-bottomed skillet over medium-high heat. When the skillet is hot, add the sesame seeds, half of the cumin seeds and the cayenne pepper; toast the seeds, stirring constantly, until the sesame seeds turn light gold — about one minute. Transfer the mixture to a large bowl and let the seeds cool.

Peel the potatoes, then cut them into slices about ⅓ inch thick, halve them, and put them in the bowl with the sesame seed mixture. Grind the remaining cumin with a mortar and pestle and sprinkle it over the potatoes. Add the peas, cucumber, scallions, lemon juice and salt to the bowl. Toss the ingredients well to combine them, and set the bowl aside.

Heat the safflower oil in a heavy-bottomed skillet over medium-high heat. When the oil is hot, reduce the heat to low and stir in the turmeric; immediately add the peppers and sauté them, stirring constantly, for one minute. Remove the pepper pieces and reserve them, and pour the contents of the skillet over the potato mixture. Stir the salad gently to blend it, then transfer it to a serving platter. Garnish the salad with the reserved peppers. The salad may be served at room temperature or chilled.

Chilies — A Cautionary Note

Both dried and fresh hot chilies should be handled with care. Their flesh and seeds contain volatile oils that can make skin tingle and cause eyes to burn. Rubber gloves offer protection — but the cook should still be careful not to touch the face, lips or eyes when working with chilies.

Soaking fresh chilies in cold, salted water for an hour will remove some of their fire. If canned chilies are substituted for fresh ones, they should be rinsed in cold water in order to eliminate as much of the brine used to preserve them as possible.

Sweet and Spicy Corn Salad

Serves 12 as a side dish
Working time: about 20 minutes
Total time: about 25 minutes

Calories **105**
Protein **2g.**
Cholesterol **0mg.**
Total fat **3g.**
Saturated fat **0g.**
Sodium **60mg.**

5 cups fresh corn kernels (cut from about 5 large ears), or 5 cups frozen corn kernels, defrosted
1 sweet red pepper, seeded, deribbed and cut into thin, 1-inch-long strips
1 green pepper, seeded, deribbed and cut into thin, 1-inch-long strips
2 small jalapeño peppers, seeded, deribbed and finely chopped (caution, above)
1 small red onion, chopped
¼ cup red wine vinegar
1 tbsp. brown sugar
2 tbsp. safflower oil
2 tsp. chopped fresh oregano, or ½ tsp. dried oregano
¼ tsp. salt
freshly ground black pepper

Pour enough water into a saucepan to fill it about 1 inch deep. Set a vegetable steamer in the pan and bring the water to a boil. Put the fresh corn into the steamer, cover the pan, and steam the corn until it is just tender—about three minutes. (Frozen corn does not require steaming.)

In a large bowl, combine the corn with the peppers and the onion. In a separate bowl, whisk together the vinegar, brown sugar, safflower oil, oregano, salt and pepper. Pour the dressing over the vegetable mixture and toss to combine. Serve the salad at room temperature, or refrigerate it for at least one hour and serve it well chilled.

Greens with Violets

VIOLET BLOSSOMS ADD A DELICIOUS DELICACY TO A SIMPLE
GREEN SALAD. PICK THE BLOSSOMS JUST BEFORE SERVING
TIME. DO NOT USE VIOLETS FROM A FLORIST — THEY MAY HAVE
BEEN SPRAYED WITH CHEMICALS.

Serves 4 as a first course or side dish
Working time: about 10 minutes
Total time: about 15 minutes

Calories **60**
Protein **1g.**
Cholesterol **0mg.**
Total fat **5g.**
Saturated fat **1g.**
Sodium **25mg.**

1 tbsp. raspberry vinegar
1 tbsp. finely chopped shallot
½ tsp. Dijon mustard
freshly ground black pepper
1½ tbsp. unsalted chicken stock
1½ tbsp. virgin olive oil
½ lb. mixed salad greens, washed and dried
¼ cup violet blossoms
¼ cup wild strawberries (optional)

Combine the vinegar, shallot, mustard and some pepper in a small bowl. Let the mixture stand for five minutes; whisk in the stock, then the oil. Toss the greens with the dressing. Strew the violets and the strawberries, if you are using them, over the top; serve the salad immediately.

EDITOR'S NOTE: *The greens shown here include escarole, Belgian endive, watercress, green-leaf lettuce and red oakleaf lettuce; any similar combination of mild and bitter greens would be appropriate, provided they are impeccably fresh.*

Salad of Fiddlehead Ferns with Pine Nuts

FIDDLEHEADS, SO NAMED FOR THEIR RESEMBLANCE TO THE SCROLL OF A VIOLIN, ARE THE TIGHTLY CURLED SHOOTS OF FERNS. THE OSTRICH FERN IS THE ONLY ONE CONSIDERED SAFE TO EAT.

Serves 4 as a first course
Working (and total) time: about 20 minutes

Calories **70**
Protein **3g.**
Cholesterol **0mg.**
Total fat **5g.**
Saturated fat **0g.**
Sodium **135mg.**

½ lb. fiddlehead ferns, washed, the brown papery husks removed
1½ tbsp. pine nuts
1 shallot, finely chopped
1 tbsp. fresh lemon juice
¼ tsp. salt
freshly ground black pepper
1 tbsp. virgin olive oil

Cook the ferns in 2 quarts of boiling water for two minutes, stirring them halfway through the cooking. Drain the ferns and cool them thoroughly under cold running water. Place the ferns in a cloth-lined bowl and chill them while you finish the salad.

Heat the pine nuts in a small, heavy-bottomed skillet over medium heat, stirring them frequently until they are lightly toasted — five to six minutes. Let the pine nuts cool, then crush 1 tablespoon of them with the side of a heavy knife and set them aside; leave the remaining pine nuts whole, for garnish.

Combine the shallot, lemon juice, crushed pine nuts, salt and some pepper in a small bowl. Whisk in the oil and set the dressing aside.

Remove the cloth from beneath the ferns. Pour the dressing over the ferns and toss well. Divide the salad among four plates, garnishing each serving with the reserved whole pine nuts.

Wrapped Salads

THIS RECIPE CALLS FOR CUTTING THE VEGETABLES INTO BÂTONNETS, FRENCH FOR "LITTLE STICKS." BÂTONNETS ARE ABOUT 1½ INCHES LONG AND ¼ INCH SQUARE.

Serves 6 as a first course
Working time: about 1 hour
Total time: about 1 hour and 45 minutes

Calories **85**
Protein **2g.**
Cholesterol **0mg.**
Total fat **4g.**
Saturated fat **0g.**
Sodium **220mg.**

2 heads of fennel, green tops removed, the bulbs cut into bâtonnets
2 turnips (about ½ lb.), peeled and cut into bâtonnets
2 zucchini (about 1 lb.), cut into bâtonnets
zest of 2 oranges
6 large Savoy cabbage leaves
1 small red onion, finely chopped
1½ tbsp. safflower oil
juice of 1 orange
2 tbsp. finely chopped fresh chervil or parsley
½ tsp. salt
freshly ground black pepper
6 sprigs fresh chervil or parsley for garnish

Bring 2 quarts of water to a boil in a large pot. Place the fennel bâtonnets in a sieve; lower the sieve partway into the boiling water and blanch the bâtonnets until they are tender but still slightly crunchy — two to three minutes. Refresh the fennel under cold running water, drain it well, and transfer it to a large bowl. Blanch the turnip bâtonnets the same way for two to three minutes; refresh them and transfer them to the bowl. Blanch the zucchini pieces for about one minute; refresh them, too, and put them in the bowl.

Use the sieve to blanch the orange zest in the boiling water for 10 seconds; refresh the zest under cold running water and drain it well. Finely chop the zest and transfer it to the bowl with the bâtonnets.

Boil the cabbage leaves in the same pot of water until they are pliable but not too soft—about 15 sec- ▶

onds. Drain the leaves; when they are cool enough to handle, use a V-shaped cut to remove the thick core from the stem end of each leaf. Set the leaves aside.

Add the onion, oil, orange juice, chopped chervil or parsley, salt and some pepper to the bowl with the bâtonnets; toss the mixture well, then refrigerate the salad for about 15 minutes.

Spread the cabbage leaves out on a work surface. Using a slotted spoon, divide the salad evenly among the leaves. Gather the edges of a leaf over its filling; gently twist the edges closed, forming a pouch. Repeat the process to enclose the other five mounds of filling.

Place the cabbage bundles in a shallow dish and pour the dressing remaining in the bowl over the top and sides of each one. Chill the salads for about 30 minutes before serving them, garnished with the chervil or parsley sprigs.

rutabaga, shallot, salt, cayenne pepper and some black pepper. Cook the mixture, stirring frequently, until the vegetables are tender but still crisp — about seven minutes. Pour the vinegar into the pan and continue cooking, stirring frequently, until almost all of the vinegar has evaporated — 1 to 2 minutes. Stir in the watercress and cook it until it has just wilted — about 30 seconds. Transfer the salad to a serving plate and let it cool just slightly before serving it.

Cucumber and Citrus Salad

Serves 4 as a side dish
Working (and total) time: about 25 minutes

Calories **80**
Protein **2g.**
Cholesterol **0mg.**
Total fat **1g.**
Saturated fat **0g.**
Sodium **135mg.**

1 large hydroponic cucumber, or 2 regular cucumbers, peeled, cut into 2-inch-long segments
1 tsp. virgin olive oil
1 tsp. chopped fresh rosemary, or ¼ tsp. crushed dried rosemary
freshly ground black pepper
1 pink grapefruit
2 navel oranges
2 tbsp. fresh lime juice
¼ cup fresh orange juice
¼ cup fresh grapefruit juice
1 tsp. red wine vinegar
¼ tsp. salt
1 scallion, cut into 2-inch-long julienne

Using an apple corer, a melon baller or a small spoon, remove the core of seeds from each cucumber segment. Slice the segments into rings about ⅛-inch thick. Toss the rings with the oil, rosemary and a generous grinding of pepper.

Working over a bowl to catch the juice, cut away the peel, white pith and outer membrane from the grape-

Carrot, Rutabaga and Watercress Salad

Serves 6 as a side dish
Working (and total) time: about 40 minutes

Calories **60**
Protein **1g.**
Cholesterol **0mg.**
Total fat **3g.**
Saturated fat **0g.**
Sodium **70mg.**

4 tsp. virgin olive oil
3 carrots, halved lengthwise, the halves cut diagonally into ¼-inch slices
1 small rutabaga (about 11 oz.), peeled and cut into bâtonnets
1 shallot, halved, the halves quartered
⅛ tsp. salt
¼ tsp. cayenne pepper
freshly ground black pepper
¼ cup cider vinegar
1 bunch of watercress, stemmed, washed and dried

Heat the oil in a large, heavy-bottomed skillet over medium heat. When the oil is hot, add the carrots,

fruit and oranges. To separate the segments from the inner membranes, slice down to the core with a sharp knife on either side of each segment; set the segments aside. Cut each grapefruit segment in half; leave the orange segments whole. Set the bowl containing the juice aside.

Arrange the cucumber slices in a large, deep plate and position the citrus segments on top. If you are preparing the salad in advance, it may be refrigerated for up to two hours at this point.

Combine the lime juice, orange juice, grapefruit juice, vinegar and salt with the reserved juice in the bowl. Pour this dressing over the salad; scatter the scallion over the top just before serving.

Asparagus and Jerusalem Artichoke Salad

Serves 4 as a first course
Working (and total) time: about 20 minutes

Calories **45**
Protein **2g.**
Cholesterol **0mg.**
Total fat **1g.**
Saturated fat **0g.**
Sodium **5mg.**

1 lemon, cut in half
¼ lb. Jerusalem artichokes (sunchokes), scrubbed well
1 lb. asparagus, trimmed, peeled and cut diagonally into 1 ½-inch lengths
1 tsp. walnut oil or virgin olive oil
1 tbsp. cut fresh dill

Make acidulated water by squeezing the juice of a lemon half into a small bowl of cold water. Peel and slice the Jerusalem artichokes, dropping them into the water as you work.

Pour enough water into a saucepan to fill it about 1 inch deep. Set a vegetable steamer in the pan and bring the water to a boil. Put the artichoke slices into the steamer, cover the pan tightly, and steam the slices until they are tender when pierced with a knife — about five minutes. Transfer the slices to a bowl and toss them with the juice of the other lemon half.

While the artichokes are steaming, cook the asparagus. Pour enough water into a large skillet to fill it about 1 inch deep. Bring the water to a boil, add the asparagus pieces, and cook them until they are tender — about four minutes. Drain the asparagus and refresh the pieces under cold running water. Drain the pieces once again and toss them with the oil.

Arrange the asparagus on a large serving platter or on four small plates. Top the asparagus with the artichoke slices; sprinkle the dill over all before serving.

Julienned Carrots, Snow Peas and Endive

Serves 6 as a first course or side dish
Working (and total) time: about 20 minutes

Calories **60**
Protein **2g.**
Cholesterol **0mg.**
Total fat **4g.**
Saturated fat **0g.**
Sodium **70mg.**

1 tbsp. very finely chopped shallot
1 garlic clove, lightly crushed
1 tbsp. herbed vinegar or white wine vinegar
1½ tbsp. almond oil or walnut oil
⅛ tsp. salt
freshly ground black pepper
¾ cup julienned carrot
1 cup julienned snow peas
2 heads of Belgian endive (about ½ lb.), cored and julienned

In a large bowl, combine the shallot, garlic and vinegar. Whisk in the oil and season the dressing with the salt and some pepper. Set the dressing aside while you prepare the vegetables.

Add the carrot julienne to 1 quart of boiling water and cook it for one minute. Add the snow peas and cook the vegetables for only 15 seconds longer. Briefly refresh the vegetables under cold running water, then drain them well. Remove the garlic from the dressing and discard it. Add the cooked vegetables and the Belgian endive to the dressing. Toss the salad well and serve it immediately.

Six-Treasure Asian Medley

Serves 10 as a side dish
Working (and total) time: about 40 minutes

Calories **70**
Protein **2g.**
Cholesterol **0mg.**
Total fat **4g.**
Saturated fat **0g.**
Sodium **220mg.**

¾ lb. carrots
¼ lb. snow peas, strings removed
2 small cucumbers, preferably unwaxed
¼ cup sliced water chestnuts
½ lb. Nappa cabbage, sliced crosswise into ½-inch-thick strips
1 sweet red pepper, seeded, deribbed and julienned
Ginger-sesame dressing
1 tsp. Sichuan peppercorns
1 tsp. dry mustard
2 tsp. sugar
3 tbsp. rice vinegar
3 tbsp. low-sodium soy sauce
2 tsp. dark sesame oil
2 tbsp. safflower oil
1 tbsp. finely chopped fresh ginger
3 garlic cloves, finely chopped

With a small paring knife or a channel knife, cut a shallow groove running the length of each carrot. Repeat the cut on the opposite side of each carrot, then slice the carrots diagonally into ovals about ⅛ inch thick. Put the pieces in a saucepan and pour in enough cold water to cover them by about 2 inches. Bring the water to a boil. Reduce the heat and simmer the carrots until they are barely tender — about two minutes. Drain the carrots and transfer them to a large bowl.

Cut a V-shaped notch in each end of each snow pea. Blanch the snow peas in boiling water for 30 seconds. Refresh the snow peas under cold running water, drain them well, and add them to the bowl with the carrots.

Peel the cucumbers, leaving four narrow strips of skin attached to each one. If you are using waxed cucumbers, peel them completely. Halve the cucumbers lengthwise; scoop out the seeds with a melon baller or a teaspoon. Cut the cucumber halves into ⅛-inch-thick slices. Add the cucumber slices, water chestnuts, cabbage and red pepper to the bowl containing the carrots and snow peas.

To prepare the dressing, put the Sichuan peppercorns into a small skillet and set it over medium-high heat. Cook the peppercorns until you see the first wisps of smoke. Transfer the peppercorns to a mortar or a small bowl and crush them with a pestle or the heel of a heavy knife. Whisk together the mustard, sugar, vinegar, soy sauce, sesame oil, safflower oil, peppercorns, ginger and garlic. Toss the vegetables with the dressing and serve at once.

Charcoal-Grilled Summer Salad

Serves 8 as a side dish
Working time: about 1 hour
Total time: about 1 hour and 30 minutes

Calories **95**
Protein **3g.**
Cholesterol **0mg.**
Total fat **5g.**
Saturated fat **1g.**
Sodium **115mg.**

1 large eggplant (about 1 lb.)
½ tsp. salt
2 zucchini (about 1 lb.)
½ tsp. virgin olive oil
freshly ground black pepper
2 sweet red peppers
½ lb. escarole or arugula, stemmed, washed and dried
4 ripe plum tomatoes, halved lengthwise
1 small red onion, very thinly sliced

Garlic-and-herb dressing

1 whole garlic bulb, the papery top cut off to expose the cloves
5 tsp. virgin olive oil
1 tbsp. fresh lemon juice
1 tbsp. chopped fresh parsley
½ tbsp. fresh thyme, or ½ tsp. dried thyme leaves
½ tbsp. chopped fresh oregano, or ½ tsp. dried oregano
⅛ tsp. salt
freshly ground black pepper
1 tbsp. walnut or safflower oil

To begin the dressing, first preheat the oven to 350° F. Place the garlic bulb on a piece of aluminum foil and drizzle ½ teaspoon of the olive oil over the exposed cloves. Fold the foil tightly around the bulb and roast the garlic until it is very soft — about one hour. Ap-

proximately halfway through the roasting time, start the coals in an outdoor grill. When the garlic bulb is cool enough to handle, remove the cloves from their skins and set them aside.

While the garlic is roasting, peel the eggplant and cut it lengthwise into eight slices. Sprinkle the ½ teaspoon of salt over the slices and let them stand for at least 30 minutes to neutralize their natural bitterness. Rinse the slices to rid them of the salt, and pat them dry with paper towels. Cut each of the zucchini lengthwise into four slices. Brush the eggplant and zucchini slices with the ½ teaspoon of olive oil. Sprinkle the vegetables with some pepper and set them aside.

When the coals are ready, place the red peppers on the grill; turn them as they scorch, until their skin is blistered on all sides — 10 to 15 minutes. Transfer the peppers to a bowl and cover it with plastic wrap; the trapped steam will loosen their skins.

Grill the eggplant and zucchini slices until they are golden brown but retain their shape — about five minutes per side. Remove the vegetables from the grill and let them cool to room temperature.

With a paring knife, peel the peppers. Seed and derib them, then quarter them lengthwise. Set the pepper pieces aside.

To finish the dressing, press the reserved garlic cloves through a sieve into a small bowl. Add the lemon juice, parsley, thyme, oregano, ⅛ teaspoon of salt and some pepper; stir well to combine the ingredients. Whisking vigorously, pour in the remaining 1½ tablespoons of olive oil in a thin, steady stream; incorporate the walnut or safflower oil the same way, and continue whisking until the dressing is thoroughly combined.

Arrange the escarole or arugula on a large platter to form a bed for the other vegetables. Position the eggplant, zucchini, red peppers, tomatoes and onion in rows on the greens. Pour the dressing over the vegetables and serve.

Shiitake Mushroom Salad

Serves 4 as a first course
Working time: about 20 minutes
Total time: about 30 minutes

Calories **95**
Protein **2g.**
Cholesterol **0mg.**
Total fat **5g.**
Saturated fat **1g.**
Sodium **150mg.**

1½ tbsp. virgin olive oil
½ cup thinly sliced shallots
½ lb. fresh shiitake mushrooms, stemmed and wiped clean, the caps sliced
2 tsp. fresh thyme, or ½ tsp. dried thyme leaves
¼ tsp. salt
2 ripe tomatoes, seeded and cut into ¼-inch-wide strips
2 tbsp. balsamic vinegar, or 1½ tbsp. red wine vinegar mixed with ½ tsp. honey
1 tbsp. fresh lemon juice
freshly ground black pepper
1 tbsp. chopped fresh parsley
4 large Nappa-cabbage leaves or romaine-lettuce leaves for garnish

Heat the olive oil in a large, heavy-bottomed skillet over medium heat. Add the shallots, mushrooms and thyme, and cook them, stirring frequently, for seven minutes. Sprinkle the contents of the pan with the salt, then stir in the tomatoes, vinegar, lemon juice and some pepper. Cook the mixture, stirring often, until the tomatoes are soft — about four minutes. Stir in the parsley and remove the skillet from the heat. Let the mixture stand until it is tepid.

Place a cabbage or lettuce leaf on each of four plates; divide the salad evenly among the leaves.

Bean Sprouts in a Sesame Vinaigrette

Serves 8 as a side dish
Working time: about 10 minutes
Total time: about 25 minutes

Calories **50**
Protein **2g.**
Cholesterol **0mg.**
Total fat **3g.**
Saturated fat **0g.**
Sodium **80mg.**

2 tbsp. Chinese black vinegar or balsamic vinegar
1 tbsp. low-sodium soy sauce
1 tbsp. safflower oil
1 tsp. dark sesame oil
1½ tsp. sugar
1 lb. fresh mung bean sprouts (technique, page 37)
1 tbsp. sesame seeds
1 scallion, trimmed and finely chopped

Bring 3 quarts of water to a boil in a large pot. While the water is heating, combine the vinegar, soy sauce, safflower oil, sesame oil and sugar in a small bowl.

Immerse the bean sprouts in the boiling water; stir them once and drain them immediately. Refresh the sprouts under cold running water, then transfer them to a bowl lined with a clean cloth; the cloth will absorb the water. Refrigerate the bean sprouts for at least 10 minutes.

Remove the cloth, leaving the sprouts in the bowl. Pour the dressing over the sprouts and toss the salad well. Chill the salad for five minutes more and toss it once again. Sprinkle the sesame seeds and chopped scallion over the top, and serve at once.

Asian-Style Cucumber Salad

Serves 6 as a side dish
Working time: about 30 minutes
Total time: about 3 hours (includes chilling)

Calories **35**
Protein **0g.**
Cholesterol **0mg.**
Total fat **3g.**
Saturated fat **0g.**
Sodium **5mg.**

2 tbsp. rice vinegar
1 garlic clove, finely chopped
1 tsp. finely chopped fresh ginger
1 tsp. mirin (sweetened Japanese rice wine)
¼ tsp. dark sesame oil
1 tbsp. peanut or safflower oil
1 hydroponic cucumber, unpeeled, or 2 regular cucumbers, peeled
¼ cup julienned carrot
¼ cup julienned yellow squash
¼ cup radish sprouts (technique, page 37)

Combine the vinegar, garlic, ginger, mirin, sesame oil, and peanut or safflower oil in a bowl. Set the vinaigrette aside.

With a channel knife or a paring knife, cut four shallow lengthwise grooves in the cucumber or cucumbers. Halve each cucumber lengthwise. (If you are using regular cucumbers, be sure to seed them.) Thinly slice the cucumber halves.

Put the cucumber, carrot, squash and radish sprouts in the vinaigrette; stir well. Refrigerate the mixture for two to three hours before serving.

A Potpourri of Vegetables Bathed in Balsamic Vinegar

Serves 8 as a first course
Working time: about 40 minutes
Total time: about 50 minutes

Calories **80**
Protein **3g.**
Cholesterol **0mg.**
Total fat **4g.**
Saturated fat **1g.**
Sodium **135mg.**

2 ½ tbsp. virgin olive oil
3 shallots, thinly sliced
1 garlic clove, finely chopped
1 bunch beet greens with stems, washed and thinly sliced (about 2 cups)
¼ tsp. salt
freshly ground black pepper
⅓ cup balsamic vinegar
2 carrots, halved lengthwise and sliced diagonally into ½-inch pieces
2 small turnips, peeled and cut into bâtonnets
2 cups small broccoli florets
2 small zucchini (about ½ lb.), halved lengthwise and sliced diagonally into ½-inch pieces
1 small yellow squash (about ¼ lb.), halved lengthwise and sliced diagonally into ½-inch pieces

Pour 3 quarts of water into a large pot; add 1 teaspoon of salt and bring the water to a boil.

In the meantime, heat 1½ tablespoons of the oil in a large, heavy-bottomed skillet set over medium heat. Add the shallots and garlic, and cook them for two minutes. Stir in the beet greens and their stems, the ¼ teaspoon of salt and some pepper. Cook the mixture, stirring frequently, for seven minutes. Pour the vinegar over the mixture, stir well, and remove the skillet from the heat.

Put the carrots into the boiling water and cook them for one minute. Add the turnips and broccoli to the carrots in the pot, and cook them for two minutes. Add the zucchini and yellow squash to the pot, and cook all the vegetables together for only 30 seconds more. Immediately drain the vegetables and refresh them under cold running water; when they are cool, drain them on paper towels.

Transfer the vegetables to a bowl and pour the contents of the skillet over them. Drizzle the remaining tablespoon of oil over the top, add a liberal grinding of pepper, and toss the salad well. Chill the salad for at least 10 minutes. Toss it once more before presenting it at the table.

Alfalfa Sprouts and
Red Onion Salad

Serves 4 as a first course
Working (and total) time: about 15 minutes

Calories **75**
Protein **1g.**
Cholesterol **0mg.**
Total fat **5g.**
Saturated fat **0g.**
Sodium **70mg.**

1 navel orange
1 tbsp. fresh lemon juice
1 tbsp. safflower oil
1 tsp. virgin olive oil
1 tsp. fresh thyme, or ¼ tsp. dried thyme leaves
½ tsp. sugar
⅛ tsp. salt
freshly ground black pepper
1 red onion, sliced into paper-thin rounds, the rings separated
1 cup alfalfa sprouts (about 1 ½ oz.)

Working over a bowl to catch the juice, cut away the peel, white pith and outer membrane from the orange. To separate the segments from the inner membranes, slice down to the core with a sharp knife on either side of each segment and set the segments aside. Squeeze the remaining membranes over the bowl to extract any juice.

Stir the lemon juice, safflower oil, olive oil, thyme, sugar, salt and some pepper into the juice in the bowl. Whisk the dressing well.

Put the onion rings into a bowl and pour half of the dressing over them. Add a generous grinding of pepper and toss well. In the other bowl, combine the alfalfa sprouts with the remaining dressing.

Spread equal amounts of the onion rings on four plates. Mound one fourth of the sprouts in the center of each bed of onions, then garnish each serving with the orange segments. Serve the salads immediately.

Tomato Fans with Basil, Ham and Provolone

Serves 4 as a first course or side dish
Working time: about 20 minutes
Total time: about 35 minutes

Calories **105**
Protein **5g.**
Cholesterol **11mg.**
Total fat **7g.**
Saturated fat **2g.**
Sodium **280mg.**

2 large, ripe tomatoes, cored
¼ tsp. sugar
⅛ tsp. salt
freshly ground black pepper
2 tbsp. sherry vinegar or red wine vinegar
1 shallot, finely chopped
1 tbsp. virgin olive oil
2 garlic cloves, crushed
1 ½ oz. thinly sliced prosciutto, julienned
2 thin slices provolone cheese (about 1 oz.), julienned
2 tbsp. thinly sliced fresh basil leaves
1 small head of Boston lettuce or 1 head of Bibb lettuce (about ¼ lb.), washed and dried

Halve the tomatoes from top to bottom, then, with the cut side down, thinly slice each half, and set it aside intact. Transfer the sliced halves to a plate. Gently fan out each half. Sprinkle the tomatoes with the sugar, salt and a generous grinding of pepper, then drizzle 1 tablespoon of the vinegar over them. Refrigerate the tomatoes for about 10 minutes.

Meanwhile, prepare the dressing. Put the shallot and the remaining 1 tablespoon of vinegar into a bowl. Whisk in the oil. Add the garlic, ham, cheese, basil and some more pepper, and stir the mixture to combine it; set it aside.

Arrange the lettuce on a serving platter and place the tomato fans on the leaves. Remove the garlic cloves from the dressing and spoon ¼ of it on each tomato fan. Serve the salad immediately.

Baby Leeks in Caper- Cream Vinaigrette

Serves 6 as a first course
Working time: about 20 minutes
Total time: about 45 minutes

Calories **190**
Protein **2g.**
Cholesterol **3mg.**
Total fat **4g.**
Saturated fat **1g.**
Sodium **200mg.**

12 baby leeks (about 1 ½ lb.), trimmed, green tops cut to within 2 inches of the white part
2 tsp. fresh thyme, or ½ tsp. dried thyme leaves
2 shallots, finely chopped
¼ tsp. salt
freshly ground black pepper
1 tbsp. fresh lemon juice
1 tbsp. red wine vinegar
1 tsp. capers, rinsed and chopped
1 tbsp. virgin olive oil
2 tbsp. light table cream
2 tbsp. chopped sweet red pepper
1 garlic clove, very finely chopped

Wash each leek to remove the grit: Without splitting the leek or detaching any leaves, gently pry apart the leaves and run cold water between them to force out the dirt. Shake the excess water from the leaves and repeat the washing process. Arrange the leeks in a skillet large enough to hold them in a single layer. Pour in just enough water to cover the leeks; add the thyme, half of the shallots, ⅛ teaspoon of the salt and a lavish grinding of pepper. Poach the leeks over medium-low heat for 10 minutes. Gently turn the leeks over, and continue poaching them until they are tender — about 10 minutes more. Transfer the leeks to a plate lined with a double thickness of paper towels. Refrigerate the leeks until they are cool — at least 20 minutes.

About 10 minutes before the leeks are sufficiently chilled, combine the remaining shallots in a small bowl with the lemon juice, vinegar, capers, the remaining ⅛ teaspoon of salt and some more pepper. Let the vinaigrette stand for five minutes, then whisk in the oil, cream, red pepper and garlic.

Transfer the cooled leeks to a serving dish. Pour the vinaigrette over the leeks and serve them at once.

Green Bean and Jícama Salad

Serves 6 as a side dish
Working time: about 20 minutes
Total time: about 35 minutes

Calories **70**
Protein **2g.**
Cholesterol **0mg.**
Total fat **4g.**
Saturated fat **1g.**
Sodium **195mg.**

½ lb. green beans, trimmed
¾ lb. jícama, peeled, and julienned or shredded
6 oil-cured black olives, thinly sliced
¼ cup sun-dried tomatoes in oil
⅔ cup warm unsalted chicken stock
1½ tbsp. red wine vinegar

Pour enough water into a saucepan to fill it about 1 inch deep. Set a vegetable steamer in the pan and bring the water to a boil. Put the green beans into the steamer, cover the pan tightly, and steam the beans until they are just tender — six to seven minutes. Remove the beans from the pan; refresh them under cold running water to preserve their color. Steam the jícama until it is just tender — two to three minutes. Refresh the jícama too.

Cut the beans diagonally into 2-inch pieces. Combine the green beans, jícama and olives in a shallow bowl, and refrigerate them for 10 to 15 minutes while you prepare the dressing.

Remove the excess oil from the tomatoes by pressing them between paper towels. Put the tomatoes, stock and vinegar into a blender or food processor. Purée the dressing, stopping once or twice to scrape down the sides. Spoon some of the dressing over the chilled vegetables and serve the salad at once, with the remaining dressing passed separately.

Dandelion Greens with Potato and Canadian Bacon

THE PLEASINGLY PUNGENT LEAVES OF DANDELION MAKE FOR A BRACING SALAD. HARVEST THE BRIGHT GREEN LEAVES IN THE SPRING; THE DARKER LEAVES THAT GROW IN THE SUMMER ARE BITTER. DANDELION GREENS ARE COMMERCIALLY AVAILABLE IN PRODUCE MARKETS FROM FEBRUARY THROUGH JUNE.

Serves 4 as a first course
Working time: about 30 minutes
Total time: about 45 minutes

Calories **130**
Protein **5g.**
Cholesterol **9mg.**
Total fat **6g.**
Saturated fat **1g.**
Sodium **265mg.**

1 large boiling potato
1 tbsp. safflower oil
1½ oz. Canadian bacon, julienned
2 shallots, thinly sliced
2 tbsp. red wine vinegar
¼ cup unsalted chicken stock
½ tsp. sugar
⅛ tsp. salt
freshly ground black pepper
½ lb. dandelion greens, washed and dried

Boil the potato until it is barely tender — about 15 minutes. Remove the potato from the water and set it aside until it is cool enough to handle. Peel the potato and cut it into small dice.

Heat the safflower oil in a heavy-bottomed skillet over medium-high heat. Add the bacon and shallots, and sauté them until the bacon begins to brown — four to five minutes. Add the diced potato and continue sautéing until the potato pieces begin to brown too — about three minutes more.

Stir in the vinegar and cook the mixture for two minutes. Add the stock, sugar, salt and some pepper; cook the mixture, stirring often, until the liquid is reduced by half — about three minutes.

Pour the contents of the skillet over the dandelion greens and toss well; serve the salad immediately.

Molded Leek Salads

Serves 4 as a first course
Working time: about 30 minutes
Total time: about 2 hours and 30 minutes

Calories **80**
Protein **6g.**
Cholesterol **2mg.**
Total fat **1g.**
Saturated fat **0g.**
Sodium **80mg.**

3 leeks (about ¾ lb.), trimmed, split, washed thoroughly to remove all grit, and sliced crosswise into ¼-inch-thick pieces
1 cup cold unsalted chicken stock
1 tbsp. fresh lemon juice
1 tbsp. unflavored powdered gelatin
½ cup plain low-fat yogurt
½ tbsp. Dijon mustard
¼ cup finely chopped fresh parsley
1 tbsp. finely cut fresh chives
freshly ground black pepper
watercress sprigs for garnish

Add the leeks to 2 quarts of water boiling in a pot. Return the water to a boil and cook the leeks until they are tender — about two minutes. Drain the leeks thoroughly and allow them to cool.

In a bowl, combine ½ cup of the stock with the lemon juice. Sprinkle the gelatin on top of the liquid and allow it to soften. Meanwhile, heat the remaining ½ cup of stock in a small saucepan over low heat. Pour the gelatin mixture into the pan, then stir gently until the gelatin dissolves. Return the gelatin mixture to the bowl and set the bowl in a larger vessel filled with ice cubes. Whisk in the yogurt and mustard. Chill the mixture, stirring it from time to time. When it begins to set — after about 20 minutes — fold in the leeks, parsley, chives and some pepper.

Rinse four ½-cup ramekins with cold water. Shake the ramekins dry, leaving a few drops of water clinging inside. Divide the leek mixture evenly among the ramekins, then chill them until the mixture is firm — about two hours.

To serve the molded salads, run the tip of a knife around the inside of each ramekin. Dip the bottoms of the ramekins in hot water for about 15 seconds, then unmold the salads onto individual plates. Garnish each one with a few sprigs of watercress and serve at once.

Escarole Chiffonade with Mild and Hot Peppers

Serves 6 as a side dish
Working time: about 20 minutes
Total time: about 45 minutes

Calories **55**
Protein **2g.**
Cholesterol **0mg.**
Total fat **4g.**
Saturated fat **1g.**
Sodium **125mg.**

½ cup unsalted veal or chicken stock
2 ancho peppers, seeded, one coarsely chopped, the other very thinly sliced
1 dried hot red pepper, seeded and crushed (caution, page 17)
1 shallot, coarsely chopped
1½ tbsp. red wine vinegar
¾ tsp. sugar
¼ tsp. salt
freshly ground black pepper
1½ tbsp. virgin olive oil
1 tbsp. fresh lime juice
1 large head of escarole (about 1½ lb.), trimmed, cut in half through the core, washed and dried

In a small skillet, combine the stock, ancho peppers, hot red pepper, shallot, vinegar, sugar, salt and some pepper. Bring the mixture to a simmer and cook it over low heat, stirring frequently, until only about 3 table-spoons of liquid remain — seven to 10 minutes.

Transfer the contents of the skillet to a blender. Add the oil and lime juice and purée the mixture to obtain a smooth dressing. Transfer the dressing to a large bowl; immediately add the sliced ancho pepper. Refrigerate the dressing until it is cool — about 15 minutes.

Lay an escarole half on a work surface cut side down and slice it into chiffonade (technique, page 51). Repeat the process with the other half. Toss the chiffonade with the dressing and serve the salad at once.

Gingery Cauliflower Salad

Serves 4 as a first course or side dish
Working time: about 20 minutes
Total time: about 45 minutes

Calories **60**
Protein **1g.**
Cholesterol **0mg.**
Total fat **4g.**
Saturated fat **0g.**
Sodium **150mg.**

1 head of cauliflower, trimmed and cut into florets
one 1-inch piece of fresh ginger, peeled and julienned
1 carrot, julienned
2 tbsp. white vinegar
½ tsp. sugar
¼ tsp. salt
⅛ tsp. cayenne pepper
1 tbsp. safflower oil
¼ tsp. dark sesame oil
1 scallion, trimmed, the green part julienned and soaked in ice water, the white part sliced diagonally into thin ovals

Mound the cauliflower florets on a heatproof plate to resemble a whole head of cauliflower. Scatter the ginger and carrot julienne over the cauliflower.

Combine the vinegar, sugar, salt and cayenne pepper in a small bowl. Whisk in the safflower oil and pour the dressing over the cauliflower.

Pour enough water into a large pot to fill it about 1 inch deep. Stand two or three small heatproof bowls in the water and set the plate with the cauliflower on top of the bowls. Cover the pot, bring the water to a boil and steam the cauliflower until it can be easily pierced with a knife — 15 to 20 minutes.

Remove the lid and let the steam dissipate. Lift the plate out of the pot and let the cauliflower stand until it cools to room temperature. Drizzle the sesame oil over the cauliflower and scatter the green and white scallion parts on top. Serve the salad at room temperature or chilled.

Sprouted Three-Bean Salad

ALTHOUGH SPROUTED MUNG BEANS ARE WIDELY AVAILABLE, SPROUTED CHICK-PEAS AND PINTO BEANS ARE NOT. TO SPROUT YOUR OWN, USE THE TECHNIQUE DESCRIBED ON PAGE 37 AND CONSULT THE TABLE FOR SPROUTING TIMES.

Serves 4 as a side dish
Working time: about 15 minutes
Total time: about 1 hour and 25 minutes (includes chilling)

Calories **80**
Protein **3g.**
Cholesterol **0mg.**
Total fat **4g.**
Saturated fat **0g.**
Sodium **180mg.**

¼ cup chopped green pepper
¼ cup thinly sliced red onion
1 garlic clove, finely chopped
2 tbsp. chopped fresh basil, or 2 tsp. dried basil
2 tbsp. white vinegar
2 tsp. sugar
¼ tsp. salt
freshly ground black pepper
½ cup sprouted chick-peas
½ cup sprouted pinto beans
⅔ cup sprouted mung beans
1 tbsp. safflower oil
1 head of green leaf lettuce, washed and dried

Bring two pots of water to a boil.

In a small bowl, combine the green pepper, onion, garlic, basil, vinegar, sugar, salt and some pepper. Set the mixture aside for at least five minutes.

Combine the sprouted chick-peas and pinto beans, and blanch them in one of the pots of boiling water until they are tender — five to seven minutes. Blanch the sprouted mung beans in the other pot until they too are tender — two to three minutes. Drain all of the beans, rinse them under cold running water, drain again, and toss them together in a bowl.

Add the oil to the vinegar mixture and stir it in well. Pour the dressing over the sprouted beans and stir to coat them. Chill the salad for one hour before serving it on a bed of lettuce.

A Home-Grown Treat

Sprouts, the germinated seeds of grains, legumes and other plants, constitute a welcome, crunchy addition to some salads — especially in winter, when the choice of fresh vegetables may be limited. Moreover, they pack a great deal of nutrition. During the sprouting process, the A, B, C and E vitamins they contain actually increase.

The range of seeds that may be sprouted is large indeed. Eight types are depicted here, including chick-peas, mung beans, and alfalfa and radish seeds, all called for by recipes in this book. When selecting seeds, choose only those that have been produced for consumption, not the garden variety, which may have been chemically treated.

Sprouts are so easy to germinate and take up so little space it is a wonder more people do not grow their own. All that is needed are the seeds, a container, and enough warmth and moisture for germination to occur. A sprouter like the compartmentalized one shown here allows for staggered sprouting times, guaranteeing a constant supply, or the production of several varieties at once. A wide-mouthed quart jar also works just fine.

If you pursue the jar method, drop in about ½ cup of the larger seeds or 2 or 3 tablespoons of the smaller ones. Add cold water in a ratio of about 4 parts water to 1 part seeds. Soak the larger seeds for eight to 10 hours; the smaller ones may need only three to six hours (chart, right). Once the soaking is over, drain off the water and rinse the seeds well. Cover the mouth of the jar with cheesecloth or mesh to allow air to enter and circulate, and gently shake the jar to distribute the seeds. Leave the jar in a warm, dark place, propped mouth down at a slight angle so that moisture can drain. Two or three times a day, fill the jar with cold water, gently swirl the contents, then drain them thoroughly.

Once the sprouts develop, they may be eaten at once or refrigerated, loosely packed in a covered container or a plastic bag, for up to five days. For added nutrition, you may wish to place sprouts bearing two little leaves in indirect light for several hours so that the leaves can turn green.

Sprouts await inclusion in salads. At top, clockwise from right: kidney, fenugreek, chick-pea and azuki sprouts. At bottom, clockwise from lower right: buckwheat, clover and radish sprouts. Mung beans spill from a bag; sprouted mung beans fill the jar.

A Sprouting Guide

	Soaking time (hours)	Sprouting time (days)	Sprout length (inches)
Alfalfa	3-6	3-5	1-2
Azuki bean	5-10	2-4	½-1½
Buckwheat	4-8	2-3	¼-½
Chick-pea	8-12	2-4	½
Clover	3-6	3-6	1-2
Fenugreek	4-8	3-6	1-2
Kidney bean	8-12	2-4	½-1
Lentil	5-8	2-4	¼-1
Mung bean	5-10	3-5	1-2
Pinto bean	8-12	3-4	½-1¼
Radish	4-8	3-5	½-2

Whisk in the oils, then the jalapeño pepper, ginger, garlic and some black pepper.

Pour all but 2 tablespoons of the dressing over the sweet potatoes and beans; add the scallions and toss well. Chill the vegetables for at least an hour.

To serve the salad, toss the cabbage with the remaining 2 tablespoons of dressing and transfer it to a serving plate. Mound the chilled vegetables on top and scatter the peanuts over all.

Artichoke Bottoms in Mango-and-Red-Onion Dressing

Serves 6 as a first course or side dish
Working time: about 40 minutes
Total time: about 1 hour

Calories **70**	
Protein **1g.**	
Cholesterol **0mg.**	8 large artichokes
Total fat **2g.**	1 lemon, cut in half
Saturated fat **0g.**	1 ripe mango, peeled, the flesh cut into small cubes
Sodium **75mg.**	1½ tbsp. fresh lemon or lime juice
	1 tbsp. red wine vinegar
	1 tbsp. virgin olive oil
	⅛ tsp. salt
	freshly ground black pepper
	½ cup chopped red onion

To prepare the artichoke bottoms, first break or cut the stem off one of the artichokes. Snap off and discard the outer leaves, starting at the base and continuing until you reach the pale yellow leaves at the core. Cut the top two thirds off the artichoke. Trim away any dark green leaf bases that remain on the artichoke bottom. Rub the artichoke all over with a lemon half to keep the artichoke from discoloring. Repeat these steps to prepare the remaining artichoke bottoms. Discard the lemon halves.

Heat ½ cup of water in a large, nonreactive skillet over low heat. Put the artichoke bottoms into the water, tightly cover the skillet, and steam the artichokes for seven minutes. Turn the artichoke bottoms over, cover the skillet again, and continue steaming them until they are tender when pierced with a knife — about seven minutes more. Transfer the artichokes to a plate and refrigerate them.

While the artichokes are cooking, prepare the dressing. Put the mango, lemon or lime juice, vinegar, oil, salt and some pepper into a food processor or blender. Purée the mixture, scraping down the sides at least once during the process. Transfer the dressing to a large bowl and stir in the onion.

When the artichokes are cool, scrape out the chokes with a spoon. Cut each artichoke into 12 wedges and stir them into the mango dressing. Chill the salad for at least 10 minutes before serving it.

Sweet Potato Salad with Peanuts

Serves 8 as a side dish
Working time: about 30 minutes
Total time: about 1 hour and 30 minutes

Calories **150**	
Protein **4g.**	1½ lb. sweet potatoes (yams), peeled, halved lengthwise and cut into ¼-inch-thick slices
Cholesterol **0mg.**	½ lb. green beans, trimmed and cut in half
Total fat **4g.**	3 scallions, trimmed and thinly sliced diagonally
Saturated fat **0g.**	1½ lb. Nappa cabbage, sliced into chiffonade (technique, page 51)
Sodium **140mg.**	2 tbsp. coarsely chopped dry-roasted unsalted peanuts
	Ginger dressing
	¼ cup rice vinegar
	1 tbsp. low-sodium soy sauce
	1 tbsp. safflower oil
	1 tsp. dark sesame oil
	1 jalapeño pepper, seeded, deribbed and finely chopped (caution, page 17)
	1 tbsp. finely chopped fresh ginger
	1 garlic clove, finely chopped
	freshly ground black pepper

To cook the sweet potatoes, pour enough water into a saucepan to fill it about 1 inch deep. Set a steamer in the pan and bring the water to a boil. Put the sweet potatoes into the steamer, cover the pan tightly, and steam the sweet potatoes until they are just tender — about 10 minutes. Transfer the sweet potatoes to a large bowl and set them aside.

Steam the beans until they are cooked but still crisp — about four minutes. Refresh the beans under cold running water to preserve their color, then add them to the bowl with the sweet potatoes.

While the beans are cooking, prepare the dressing: Combine the vinegar and soy sauce in a small bowl.

Endive Salad with Orange and Rosemary

Serves 6 as a first course or side dish
Working (and total) time: about 25 minutes

Calories **70**
Protein **2g.**
Cholesterol **0mg.**
Total fat **4g.**
Saturated fat **1g.**
Sodium **105mg.**

1 garlic clove, cut in half
1 head of curly endive (chicory), washed and dried
3 small heads of Belgian endive, washed, dried and sliced crosswise into ½-inch-wide strips
1 navel orange
1 small red onion, thinly sliced
1 tbsp. chopped fresh rosemary, or 1 tsp. dried rosemary, crumbled
⅛ tsp. salt
2 tbsp. sherry vinegar or red wine vinegar
1 tbsp. grainy mustard
1½ tbsp. virgin olive oil

Rub the inside of a salad bowl with the cut surfaces of the garlic clove. Put all the endive leaves in the bowl.

Working over a bowl to catch the juice, cut away the peel, white pith and outer membrane from the flesh of the orange. To separate the segments from the membranes, slice down to the core with a sharp knife on either side of each segment and set the segments aside. Cut each segment in thirds and add them to the bowl along with the onion and rosemary.

In a small bowl, whisk together the salt, reserved orange juice, vinegar and mustard. Whisking constantly, pour in the oil in a thin, steady stream to create an emulsified dressing. Pour the dressing over the contents of the salad bowl; toss the salad thoroughly and serve it at once.

Belgian Endive and Watercress Salad

Serves 6 as a first course or side dish
Working (and total) time: about 30 minutes

Calories **70**
Protein **2g.**
Cholesterol **0mg.**
Total fat **5g.**
Saturated fat **1g.**
Sodium **140mg.**

2 heads of Belgian endive
1 bunch of watercress, stemmed, washed and dried
12 mushrooms, stems trimmed, caps wiped clean and thinly sliced
18 cherry tomatoes, halved
Dill-mustard vinaigrette
1 tbsp. herb-flavored mustard or Dijon mustard
1½ tbsp. fresh lemon juice
3 scallions, trimmed, the green parts reserved for another use, the white parts finely chopped
2 tbsp. finely cut fresh dill, or 1½ tbsp. dried dill
¼ tsp. salt
freshly ground black pepper
1 tbsp. safflower oil
1 tbsp. virgin olive oil

To make the vinaigrette, combine the mustard, lemon juice, scallions, dill, salt and some pepper in a small bowl. Whisking vigorously, pour in the safflower oil in a thin, steady stream; incorporate the olive oil the same way. Set the vinaigrette aside.

Separate the endive leaves from their cores. Arrange the endive leaves, watercress, mushrooms and tomatoes on individual plates. Spoon the vinaigrette over the salads and serve them immediately.

Brussels Sprouts in Basil-Yogurt Dressing

THE TECHNIQUE OF SCULPTING VEGETABLES IN THE SHAPE OF
SMALL MUSHROOMS IS DEMONSTRATED ON PAGE 43.

Serves 4 as a first course or side dish
Working time: about 25 minutes
Total time: about 1 hour

Calories **85**
Protein **4g.**
Cholesterol **2mg.**
Total fat **1g.**
Saturated fat **1g.**
Sodium **75mg.**

¾ lb. Brussels sprouts, quartered
1 small rutabaga (about ½ lb.), cut into mushrooms, the mushrooms sliced in half
2 turnips, cut into mushrooms, the mushrooms sliced in half
Basil-yogurt dressing
2 tbsp. sweet sherry
1 garlic clove, finely chopped
1 tbsp. chopped fresh basil, or 1 tsp. dried basil
1 tsp. Dijon mustard
⅓ cup plain low-fat yogurt
2 tsp. sour cream
1 tbsp. finely chopped scallion
white pepper
several radicchio or romaine-lettuce leaves, washed and dried

Pour enough water into a saucepan to fill it about 1 inch deep. Set a vegetable steamer in the pan and bring the water to a boil. Put the Brussels sprouts into the steamer, cover the pan tightly, and steam the sprouts until they are tender — about five minutes. Transfer the sprouts to a large bowl and set them aside. Steam the rutabaga and turnip mushrooms until they are tender — six to seven minutes — and transfer them to the bowl with the Brussels sprouts.

While the vegetables are steaming, prepare the dressing. Combine the sherry, garlic and basil in a small saucepan. Simmer the mixture over medium heat until only 1 tablespoon of liquid remains — two to three minutes. Transfer the mixture to a small bowl; stir in the mustard, then the yogurt, sour cream, scallion and some white pepper.

Pour the dressing over the vegetables and toss the mixture well. Cover the bowl and chill the salad for about 20 minutes. Mound the salad on the radicchio or lettuce leaves just before serving.

Making "Mushrooms" from Root Vegetables

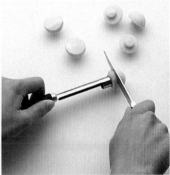

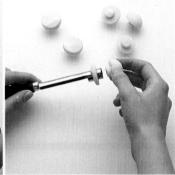

1 SCOOPING OUT ROUNDS. Slice off the top and bottom of the vegetable (here, a rutabaga) and pare it. With a large melon baller, dig deeply into the edge and scoop out as many rounds as the vegetable will yield.

2 INSERTING THE CORER. To make the stem, place a round on the work surface with the flat end upturned. Push the cutting edge of a fruit corer into the center of the flat end, about ½ inch deep.

3 TRIMMING THE PIECE. With the round still attached to the corer, cut through to the corer with a paring knife. Slowly rotating the corer, hold the knife in place until a cut has been made around the piece.

4 SEPARATING THE MUSHROOM. Carefully separate the cut piece from the round by prying it loose with the knife blade. Then grip the top of the round with your fingertips and pull out the mushroom.

Broccoli and Nappa Cabbage Salad with Black-Vinegar Dressing

Serves 8 as a side dish
Working (and total) time: about 25 minutes

Calories **40**
Protein **2g.**
Cholesterol **0mg.**
Total fat **2g.**
Saturated fat **0g.**
Sodium **120mg.**

2 broccoli stalks, the florets separated from the stems, the stems peeled and sliced diagonally
1 daikon radish
10 oz. Nappa cabbage, sliced into ½-inch pieces (about 2 cups)
1 tbsp. safflower oil
¼ tsp. dark sesame oil
Black-vinegar dressing
2 cups unsalted chicken stock
4 thin slices peeled fresh ginger
1 tsp. Sichuan peppercorns
¼ tsp. sugar
2 tbsp. Chinese black vinegar or balsamic vinegar
1 tbsp. low-sodium soy sauce

To make the dressing, first pour the stock into a small saucepan set over medium-high heat. Add the ginger, peppercorns and sugar, and bring the liquid to a boil. Cook the mixture until it is reduced to about ½ cup — 10 to 12 minutes.

While the stock is reducing, cook the broccoli. Pour enough water into a saucepan to fill it about 1 inch deep. Set a vegetable steamer in the water and add the broccoli florets and stems. Cover the pan tightly, bring the water to a boil, and steam the broccoli until it is barely tender — about two minutes. Transfer the broccoli to a bowl and refrigerate it until serving time.

Remove the reduced stock from the heat and let it cool. Stir in the vinegar and soy sauce, then strain the dressing into a small serving bowl.

Slice the daikon radish into 2-inch lengths. Stand one of the pieces on end; using a small, sharp knife, cut down the sides to remove the peel, giving the radish five sides. Repeat the process to fashion the remaining radish pieces. Thinly slice the pieces; keep them in ice water until serving time.

Drain the radish slices, pat them dry with paper towels, and transfer them to a large bowl along with the broccoli and cabbage. Combine the safflower oil and sesame oil; drizzle the oils over the vegetables and toss well. Serve the salad at once, passing the dressing separately.

Sweet Potato Salad with Curried Yogurt Dressing

Serves 6 as a side dish
Working time: about 30 minutes
Total time: about 2 hours (includes chilling)

Calories **120**
Protein **3g.**
Cholesterol **2mg.**
Total fat **1g.**
Saturated fat **0g.**
Sodium **60mg.**

1 lb. sweet potatoes (yams)
4 celery stalks, thinly sliced
3 scallions, trimmed and thinly sliced
½ cup yogurt dressing (recipe, page 13) mixed with 1 ½ tsp. curry powder
1 tbsp. each finely cut fresh chives and chopped fresh parsley, or 2 tbsp. chopped fresh parsley

Put the sweet potatoes in a deep saucepan and pour in enough water to cover them. Bring the water to a boil and cook the sweet potatoes over medium heat until they are tender — 25 to 30 minutes. Drain the sweet potatoes; when they are cool enough to handle, peel them and cut them into small dice. Put the sweet potatoes in a bowl with the celery and scallions.

Add the dressing to the vegetables and mix gently. Chill the salad for at least one hour. Just before serving, sprinkle the fresh herbs over the top.

EDITOR'S NOTE: *This salad makes a delicious accompaniment to grilled chicken or pork.*

Chayote Fans in a Cilantro Vinaigrette

Serves 4 as a first course
Working time: about 25 minutes
Total time: about 45 minutes

Calories **60**
Protein **1g.**
Cholesterol **0mg.**
Total fat **4g.**
Saturated fat **0g.**
Sodium **80mg.**

1 large chayote squash (about ¾ lb.), quartered and seeded
1 lemon
1 tbsp. red wine vinegar
½ tsp. Dijon mustard
1 tbsp. safflower oil
1 tbsp. chopped cilantro
½ tsp. sugar
⅛ tsp. salt
freshly ground black pepper
1 large dried ancho chili, cut in half lengthwise and seeded
4 cilantro sprigs for garnish

Cut a chayote quarter lengthwise into thin slices, leaving the slices attached at the tapered end to form a fan. Repeat the process with the other quarters.

Pour enough water into a saucepan to fill it about 1 inch deep. Set a vegetable steamer in the pan and bring the water to a boil. Set the chayote fans in the steamer, cover the pan, and steam the squash until it is barely tender — four to five minutes. Transfer the squash to a shallow bowl.

Cut the lemon in half. Slice one half into four rounds and reserve the rounds for garnish. Squeeze enough juice from the other half to measure 1 tablespoon and pour it into a small mixing bowl. Add the vinegar and mustard, and whisk in the oil. Season the vinaigrette with the cilantro, sugar, salt and some pepper. Pour the vinaigrette over the chayote fans and chill them.

While the squash is refrigerating, place the chili pepper in a small bowl, pour 1 cup of boiling water over it, and let it soak for 20 minutes. Remove the chili pepper from its soaking liquid; do not discard the liquid. Put the pepper pieces in a blender along with ¼ cup of the soaking liquid. Drain the vinaigrette from the chilled squash and add it to the pepper pieces and liquid. Purée the dressing and strain it through a fine sieve.

Spoon the dressing onto four individual salad plates. Transfer the chayote fans to the plates and place a sprig of cilantro on each fan. Garnish each salad with a lemon round.

Zucchini, Jícama and Apple in Rice Vinegar

Serves 8 as a side dish
Working (and total) time: about 20 minutes

Calories **30**	
Protein **1g.**	1 zucchini (about 8 oz.), julienned
Cholesterol **0mg.**	¼ lb. jícama, peeled and julienned
Total fat **1g.**	1 red apple, quartered, cored and thinly sliced
Saturated fat **0g.**	1 tsp. chopped fresh tarragon, or ½ tsp. dried tarragon
Sodium **35mg.**	1 tsp. safflower oil
	2 tbsp. rice vinegar
	⅛ tsp. salt
	freshly ground black pepper

In a large bowl, combine the zucchini, jícama, apple and tarragon. Add the oil and toss the mixture to coat the vegetables. Stir in the vinegar, salt and some pepper; toss the salad and serve it at once.

Kohlrabi Salad

Serves 6 as a side dish
Working (and total) time: about 40 minutes

Calories **45**
Protein **3g.**
Cholesterol **3mg.**
Total fat **2g.**
Saturated fat **0g.**
Sodium **45mg.**

1 lb. kohlrabies or turnips, peeled and shredded
¼ cup diced pimiento
1 tbsp. fresh lemon juice
½ cup yogurt dressing (recipe, page 13)

Pour 2 quarts of cold water into a saucepan. Add the kohlrabi or turnip shreds, bring the water to a boil, then blanch for 2 minutes. Drain them in a colander, refresh them under cold running water, and drain them again. Rid the vegetables of excess moisture by pressing down on them with the back of a large spoon. (Alternatively, wrap the vegetables in cheesecloth and wring out the water.)

Transfer the kohlrabi or turnip shreds to a bowl and stir in the pimiento and lemon juice. Pour the dressing over the top, toss the salad well, and serve it at once.

Mustard Greens with Red Potatoes and Apple

Serves 8 as a side dish
Working time: about 25 minutes
Total time: about 1 hour and 25 minutes

Calories **105**
Protein **2g.**
Cholesterol **2mg.**
Total fat **3g.**
Saturated fat **1g.**
Sodium **150mg.**

1 large tart apple, preferably Stayman or Winesap
1 tbsp. fresh lemon juice
1 lb. red potatoes, scrubbed and cut into ¾-inch cubes
½ tsp. salt
1 tbsp. red wine vinegar
1½ tbsp. virgin olive oil
1 shallot, finely chopped
½ lb. mustard greens or young kale, stemmed, washed, torn into 2-inch pieces and dried
½ cup whole milk
freshly ground black pepper

Peel, quarter and core the apple, and cut it into ¾-inch pieces. In a small bowl, toss the apple with the lemon juice; set the bowl aside.

Pour 2 cups of water into a saucepan. Add the potatoes and salt, and bring the water to a boil. Reduce the heat and simmer the potatoes for 10 minutes. Add the apple and continue cooking the mixture, stirring often so that it does not burn, until only 2 tablespoons of liquid remain — about 10 minutes more.

Combine the vinegar and ½ tablespoon of the oil in a small bowl. Pour this mixture over the hot potatoes and apple, and set them aside.

Heat the remaining tablespoon of oil in a large, heavy-bottomed skillet over medium heat. Cook the shallot in the oil for one minute. Add the greens and cook them, stirring frequently, until they are wilted — about three minutes. Pour in the milk and continue cooking the mixture until all the liquid has evaporated — seven to 10 minutes.

Combine the potato mixture, the greens and a generous grinding of pepper in a large bowl. Toss the salad well and refrigerate it for at least 45 minutes. Toss it once more before serving.

Green Beans with Creamy Horseradish Dressing

Serves 8 as a first course
Working time: about 40 minutes
Total time: about 1 hour and 15 minutes

Calories **55**
Protein **3g.**
Cholesterol **1mg.**
Total fat **1g.**
Saturated fat **0g.**
Sodium **115mg.**

2 sweet red peppers
8 artichokes
1 lemon, halved
½ lb. green beans, trimmed
½ lb. okra, trimmed
Horseradish dressing
½ cup plain low-fat yogurt
¼ cup prepared horseradish, drained
1 tsp. celery seeds
1 tsp. fresh lemon juice
¼ tsp. salt
1 tbsp. chopped fresh thyme, or 1 tsp. dried thyme leaves
3 tbsp. chopped fresh parsley
⅛ tsp. cayenne pepper
freshly ground black pepper

Roast the peppers about 2 inches below a preheated broiler, turning them until their skin has blistered on all sides. Transfer the peppers to a bowl and cover it with plastic wrap; the trapped steam will loosen their skins. When the peppers are cool enough to handle, peel, seed and derib them, and cut them into ¼-inch cubes.

To prepare each artichoke bottom, first break or cut off the stem. Snap off and discard the outer leaves, starting at the base and continuing until you reach the pale yellow leaves at the core. Cut the top two thirds off the artichoke. Trim away any dark green leaf bases that remain on the artichoke bottom. Rub the artichoke all over with one of the lemon halves.

Fill a large, nonreactive saucepan with water and bring it to a boil. Squeeze the juice of both lemon halves into the water, then add the lemon halves themselves. Add the artichoke bottoms to the boiling water and cook them until they can be easily pierced with the tip of a sharp knife — about 15 minutes. Drain the artichoke bottoms and refresh them under cold running water. Using a teaspoon, scrape the furry choke from each artichoke bottom. Rinse and drain the bottoms, and cut each one into eight pieces.

Pour enough water into a large saucepan to fill it about 1 inch deep. Set a vegetable steamer in the pan and bring the water to a boil. Put the green beans into the steamer, cover the pan tightly, and steam the beans until they are tender — about six minutes. Lift out the steamer; refresh the beans under cold running water, then drain them well, and set them aside.

Return the steamer to the pan and bring the water to a boil. Set the okra in the steamer, cover the pan tightly, and steam the okra until it is barely tender — about three minutes. Remove the okra from the pan and refresh it under cold running water. Cut each okra in half lengthwise and set it aside.

To prepare the dressing, whisk together the yogurt, horseradish, celery seeds, lemon juice, salt, thyme, parsley, cayenne pepper and some black pepper in a large bowl. Add the beans, artichoke bottoms, okra and all but 2 tablespoons of the red peppers to the dressing. Toss well and serve the salad with the reserved red pepper cubes sprinkled on top.

EDITOR'S NOTE: *Provided it is stored in the refrigerator, the dressing may be made a day in advance.*

Carrot and Orange Salad with Dill

Serves 4 as a side dish
Working time: about 10 minutes
Total time: about 25 minutes

Calories **90**
Protein **2g.**
Cholesterol **0mg.**
Total fat **0g.**
Saturated fat **0g.**
Sodium **50mg.**

1 navel orange
6 carrots (about 1¼ lb.), finely grated
1 tbsp. red wine vinegar
½ cup fresh orange juice
½ tsp. grated orange zest
2 tbsp. fresh dill

Working over a bowl to catch the juice, cut away the peel, white pith and outer membrane from the orange. To separate the segments from the inner membranes, slice down to the core with a sharp knife on either side of each segment and set the segments aside.

Combine the carrots, vinegar, orange juice and zest in the bowl. Add the orange segments and 1 tablespoon of the dill; gently toss the ingredients. Refrigerate the salad for at least 15 minutes. Shortly before serving, garnish the top with the remaining dill.

Red, White and Green Salad

Serves 6 as a first course or side dish
Working time: about 20 minutes
Total time: about 1 hour

Calories **60**
Protein **2g.**
Cholesterol **0mg.**
Total fat **4g.**
Saturated fat **0g.**
Sodium **75mg.**

1 beet (about ½ lb.), rinsed
3 tbsp. raspberry vinegar or red wine vinegar
2 tsp. Dijon mustard
2 tsp. grainy mustard
¼ tsp. honey
freshly ground black pepper
1 ½ tbsp. virgin olive oil

1 head of radicchio, halved, cored, washed, dried and cut into chiffonade (technique, page 51)
1 large head of Belgian endive, cored, cut in half crosswise, the halves julienned
¼ lb. mâche (corn salad or lamb's lettuce), washed and dried, or 1 small head of Boston or Bibb lettuce, washed, dried and torn into pieces

Put the beet into a saucepan, pour in enough water to cover the beet, and bring the water to a boil. Cook the beet until it is tender — about 30 minutes. Drain the beet and let it cool before peeling and finely dicing it.

Put the diced beet in a small bowl, and toss it with 1 tablespoon of the vinegar.

To make the dressing, combine the mustards, the honey, the remaining 2 tablespoons of vinegar and a liberal grinding of pepper in a bowl. Whisk in the oil.

In another bowl, toss the radicchio and endive with two thirds of the dressing. Separately toss the mâche or lettuce with the remaining dressing.

To assemble the salad, mound the radicchio-endive mixture in the center of a platter and surround it with the mâche or lettuce. Scatter the diced beet on top.

Cutting Chiffonade

1 *ROLLING THE LEAVES. Pluck the leaves from a head of spinach, lettuce or cabbage (here, radicchio). Gently wash and dry the leaves. Stack three to four leaves and roll them into a bundle.*

2 *CUTTING THE ROLL. Holding the bundle with your fingers curled under for safety, square the end by cutting off the rounded tips of the leaves. Slice across the roll at approximately ⅛-inch intervals to produce the thin strips called chiffonade.*

Spinach and Sesame Salad

Serves 6 as a side dish
Working (and total) time: about 30 minutes

Calories **60**
Protein **4g.**
Cholesterol **0mg.**
Total fat **5g.**
Saturated fat **0g.**
Sodium **255mg.**

½ cup unsalted chicken stock
1 tbsp. hulled sesame seeds
1 tbsp. tahini (sesame paste)
1 tsp. dark sesame oil
1½ tbsp. low-sodium soy sauce
1 tbsp. fresh lemon juice
1 tsp. finely chopped fresh ginger
1 lb. spinach, washed, stemmed and dried
¼ lb. mushrooms, wiped clean and thinly sliced (about 1 cup)
1 large ripe tomato, sliced into thin wedges
⅛ tsp. salt
freshly ground black pepper

Boil the stock in a small saucepan until only 2 tablespoons remain — about seven minutes.

While the stock is reducing, toast the sesame seeds in a small, heavy-bottomed skillet over medium-low heat until they are golden — about three minutes. Set the skillet aside.

To prepare the dressing, mix the tahini and sesame oil in a small bowl. Whisk in the reduced stock, the soy sauce, lemon juice and ginger.

Put the spinach and mushrooms into a large bowl. Sprinkle the tomato wedges with the salt and pepper and add them to the bowl. Pour the dressing over the vegetables, grind in some more pepper, and toss well. Scatter the sesame seeds over the salad and serve.

Kale, Pear and Goat-Cheese Salad

Serves 8 as a first course
Working (and total) time: about 40 minutes

Calories **90**
Protein **4g.**
Cholesterol **5mg.**
Total fat **4g.**
Saturated fat **1g.**
Sodium **200mg.**

1 ½ tbsp. virgin olive oil
3 onions (about 1 lb.), thinly sliced
¼ tsp. salt
1 lb. kale, stemmed and washed, the large leaves torn in half
½ cup cider vinegar
2 oz. thinly sliced pancetta (Italian bacon) or prosciutto, cut into thin strips
1 Comice or Bartlett pear, quartered, cored and thinly sliced lengthwise
freshly ground black pepper
2 oz. fresh goat cheese, broken into small pieces

Heat 1 tablespoon of the olive oil in a large, heavy-bottomed skillet over medium heat. Add the onions and ⅛ teaspoon of the salt; cook the onions, scraping the browned bits from the bottom of the pan vigorously and often, until the onions are caramelized — 25 to 30 minutes.

Meanwhile, cook the kale in 3 quarts of boiling water for seven minutes. Drain the kale and refresh it under cold running water. When the kale has cooled thoroughly, mold it into a ball and squeeze out as much liquid as possible.

When the onions are caramelized, stir the vinegar into the skillet, scraping up any remaining pan deposits. Continue cooking the mixture until most of the liquid has evaporated — about five minutes.

Heat the remaining ½ tablespoon of oil in a smaller skillet over medium heat. Cook the pancetta or prosciutto in the oil for one minute, add it to the onion mixture, then stir in the kale, the pear, the remaining ⅛ teaspoon of salt and a generous grinding of pepper. Stir in half of the goat cheese.

Divide the salad among eight plates; dot the tops of the portions with the remaining cheese and serve the salads immediately.

Chilled Celeriac, Carrot and Yellow Pepper Salad

Serves 6 as a side dish
Working time: about 15 minutes
Total time: about 1 hour and 15 minutes

Calories **45**
Protein **1g.**
Cholesterol **0mg.**
Total fat **2g.**
Saturated fat **0g.**
Sodium **90mg.**

½ lb. celeriac (celery root), scrubbed
2 tbsp. red wine vinegar
1 carrot, peeled and julienned
1 yellow pepper, seeded, deribbed and cut into thin strips
1 tbsp. safflower oil
¼ tsp. sugar
⅛ tsp. salt

Peel and julienne the celeriac. To prevent the pieces from discoloring, transfer them to a bowl and sprinkle them with the vinegar; toss the pieces well to coat them. Add the carrot, yellow pepper, oil, sugar and salt, and toss the mixture thoroughly to combine all the ingredients. Cover the bowl and refrigerate the salad for at least one hour before serving.

Leaves of Boston Lettuce in a Garlicky Vinaigrette

Serves 6 as a first course or side dish
Working time: about 10 minutes
Total time: about 25 minutes

Calories **110**
Protein **3g.**
Cholesterol **0mg.**
Total fat **5g.**
Saturated fat **1g.**
Sodium **150mg.**

1 whole garlic bulb, the cloves separated and peeled
1 tbsp. balsamic vinegar, or 1 tbsp. red wine vinegar mixed with ¼ tsp. honey
1 tbsp. virgin olive oil
1 tbsp. safflower oil
⅛ tsp. salt
freshly ground black pepper
2 heads of Boston lettuce, or 4 heads of Bibb lettuce, washed and dried
12 thin French-bread slices, toasted

Put the garlic cloves into a small saucepan and pour in enough water to cover them. Bring the liquid to a boil, then reduce the heat, and simmer the garlic until it is quite tender — about 15 minutes. Increase the heat and boil the liquid until only about 2 tablespoons remain — two to three minutes.

Pour the contents of the saucepan into a sieve set over a small bowl. With a wooden spoon, mash the garlic through the sieve into the bowl. Whisk the vinegar into the garlic mixture, then incorporate the olive oil, safflower oil, salt and some pepper.

Toss the lettuce leaves with the dressing; garnish the salad with the toast and serve at once.

Potato Salad with Roasted Red Pepper Sauce

Serves 8 as a side dish
Working (and total) time: about 40 minutes

Calories **110**
Protein **2g.**
Cholesterol **0mg.**
Total fat **4g.**
Saturated fat **0g.**
Sodium **70mg.**

1½ lb. round red potatoes or other boiling potatoes, scrubbed
2 sweet red peppers
2 garlic cloves, peeled and crushed
1 tsp. chopped fresh rosemary, or ½ tsp. dried rosemary, crumbled
¼ tsp. salt
cayenne pepper
2 tbsp. red wine vinegar
2 tbsp. virgin olive oil
6 oz. arugula, washed and dried, or 2 bunches watercress, stemmed, washed and dried

Put the potatoes into a large saucepan and cover them with cold water. Bring the water to a boil and cook the potatoes until they are tender when pierced with the tip of a sharp knife — about 25 minutes. Drain the potatoes and set them aside to cool.

While the potatoes are boiling, roast the peppers

about 2 inches below a preheated broiler, turning them often, until they are blistered on all sides. Put the peppers into a bowl and cover the bowl with plastic wrap; the trapped steam will loosen their skins. Peel the peppers, then seed and derib them. Put the peppers into a food processor or a blender along with the garlic, rosemary, salt and a pinch of cayenne pepper. Purée the mixture to obtain a smooth sauce. With the motor still running, pour in the vinegar, then the oil; continue blending the sauce until it is well combined.

Cut the potatoes in half and then into wedges. Arrange the wedges on a bed of arugula leaves or watercress. Pour some of the sauce over the potatoes and serve the rest alongside.

Broiled Eggplant with Mint

Serves 6 as a side dish
Working time: about 25 minutes
Total time: about 50 minutes

Calories **70**
Protein **2g.**
Cholesterol **0mg.**
Total fat **3g.**
Saturated fat **0g.**
Sodium **190mg.**

1 lb. eggplant, cut into 1-inch cubes
½ tsp. salt
2 tbsp. balsamic vinegar, or 1½ tbsp. red wine vinegar mixed with ½ tsp. honey
¼ lb. mushrooms, wiped clean and quartered
juice of ½ lemon
2 ripe tomatoes, peeled, seeded and cut into strips
1 tbsp. sliced fresh mint leaves
Peppery orange dressing
juice of 1 orange
juice of 1 lemon
1 garlic clove, finely chopped
⅛ tsp. crushed hot red-pepper flakes
¼ tsp. salt
1 tbsp. virgin olive oil

Toss the eggplant cubes with the salt and let them stand for 30 minutes to make them less bitter. Rinse the cubes and pat them dry with paper towels.

Preheat the broiler. Put the eggplant cubes into a flameproof dish and broil them, stirring often, until they are browned — about five minutes. Transfer the eggplant cubes to a bowl and mix in the vinegar. Set the bowl aside.

Put the mushrooms into a nonreactive saucepan with the lemon juice; pour in enough water to cover the mushrooms and simmer them over medium heat for about five minutes. Set the saucepan aside.

To make the dressing, combine the orange juice, lemon juice, garlic, red-pepper flakes and salt in a small saucepan. Bring the mixture to a boil and cook it until the liquid is reduced by half — about five minutes. Remove the pan from the heat and whisk in the oil.

Arrange the eggplant and tomatoes on a large plate. Drain the mushrooms and scatter them over the tomatoes. Pour the dressing over the vegetables, then sprinkle the fresh mint on top. Serve the salad at room temperature.

Fava Bean Salad

Serves 6 as a first course or side dish
Working time: about 40 minutes
Total time: about 50 minutes

Calories **125**
Protein **6g.**
Cholesterol **3mg.**
Total fat **3g.**
Saturated fat **1g.**
Sodium **95mg.**

2 tsp. virgin olive oil
1 large onion, thinly sliced
1 large garlic clove, finely chopped
2½ lb. fresh fava beans, shelled and peeled (about 2 cups), or 2 cups frozen lima beans, defrosted
2 paper-thin slices of prosciutto (about 1 oz.), julienned
1½ lb. ripe tomatoes, peeled, seeded and coarsely chopped, or 14 oz. canned unsalted tomatoes, chopped, with their juice
1 cup unsalted chicken stock, or ½ cup unsalted chicken stock if canned tomatoes are used
1 tbsp. chopped fresh oregano, or 1 tsp. dried oregano
½ tsp. cracked black peppercorns
2 tbsp. balsamic vinegar, or 1½ tbsp. red wine vinegar mixed with ½ tsp. honey

Heat the oil in a heavy-bottomed skillet over medium heat. Add the onion slices and cook them until they are translucent — four to five minutes. Stir in the garlic and cook the mixture for one minute more. Add the beans, prosciutto, tomatoes, stock, oregano and peppercorns. Bring the liquid to a simmer and cook the mixture until the beans are just tender — eight to 10 minutes. Transfer the salad to a bowl and refrigerate it.

When the salad is cool, pour in the vinegar, toss well, and serve at once.

Green Bean Salad with Gruyère and Grainy Mustard

Serves 6 as a first course or side dish
Working time: about 15 minutes
Total time: about 30 minutes

Calories **70**
Protein **3g.**
Cholesterol **8mg.**
Total fat **5g.**
Saturated fat **2g.**
Sodium **120mg.**

¾ lb. thin green beans, trimmed and cut in half diagonally
1 shallot, finely chopped
1½ tbsp. grainy mustard, or 1 tbsp. Dijon mustard
3 tbsp. red wine vinegar
1 tbsp. virgin olive oil
⅛ tsp. salt
freshly ground black pepper
1½ oz. Gruyère cheese, julienned (about ⅓ cup)

Pour enough water into a large saucepan to fill it about 1 inch deep. Set a vegetable steamer in the pan and bring the water to a boil. Put the beans into the steamer, cover the pan, and cook the beans until they are just tender — seven to eight minutes. Refresh the beans under cold running water; when they are cool, drain them on paper towels.

Mix the shallot, mustard, vinegar, oil, salt and some pepper in a large bowl. Add the cheese and green beans, and toss the beans well. Refrigerate the salad for 10 minutes. Toss it once again just before serving.

Summer Vegetables in Tomato Aspic

Serves 16 as a side dish
Working time: about 30 minutes
Total time: about 4 hours and 30 minutes
(includes chilling)

Calories **50**
Protein **3g.**
Cholesterol **0mg.**
Total fat **1g.**
Saturated fat **0g.**
Sodium **50mg.**

1½ cups fresh corn kernels (cut from 2 small ears), or 1½ cups frozen corn kernels, defrosted
28 oz. canned unsalted tomatoes, puréed in a food processor or blender
1 hydroponic cucumber, seeded and chopped, or 2 regular cucumbers, peeled, seeded and chopped
½ sweet red pepper, seeded, deribbed and chopped
½ green pepper, seeded, deribbed and chopped
1 small onion, finely chopped
1 tbsp. red wine vinegar
1 tbsp. virgin olive oil
6 drops hot red-pepper sauce

¼ tsp. celery seeds
¼ tsp. salt
freshly ground black pepper
2 tbsp. powdered unflavored gelatin
1½ cups cold unsalted chicken or vegetable stock
1 head of Boston lettuce, or 2 heads of Bibb lettuce, washed and dried

If you are using fresh corn, pour enough water into a saucepan to fill it about 1 inch deep. Set a vegetable steamer in the pan and bring the water to a boil. Put the fresh corn into the steamer; frozen corn does not require steaming. Tightly cover the pan and steam the corn for three minutes.

In a large bowl, combine the puréed tomatoes, the cucumber, red and green pepper, onion, corn, vinegar,

oil, red-pepper sauce, celery seeds, salt and some pepper. Set the bowl aside.

Stir the gelatin into ½ cup of the stock and set the mixture aside for a minute or two. Bring the remaining cup of stock to a boil, then remove it from the heat; add the gelatin-stock mixture and stir until the gelatin is dissolved.

Add the gelatin and stock to the vegetables and stir well to distribute the gelatin evenly. Pour the mixture into an 8-cup mold and chill it until it is firm — at least four hours.

Shortly before serving the salad, run the tip of a knife around the inside of the mold to loosen the sides. Briefly dip the bottom of the mold in hot water. Invert a plate on top of the mold, then turn both over together; if necessary, rap the bottom of the mold to free the salad. Lift away the mold and garnish the salad with the lettuce. Serve the salad immediately.

Broccoli Salad with Oven-Roasted Mushrooms

Serves 8 as a first course or side dish
Working (and total) time: about 1 hour and 15 minutes

Calories **105**
Protein **6g.**
Cholesterol **0mg.**
Total fat **4g.**
Saturated fat **0g.**
Sodium **150mg.**

2 lb. mushrooms, wiped clean, the stems trimmed
4 large shallots, thinly sliced lengthwise
⅓ cup fresh lemon juice
2½ tbsp. fresh thyme, or 2 tsp. dried thyme leaves
¼ tsp. salt
freshly ground black pepper
1 tbsp. safflower oil
2½ lb. broccoli, stemmed and cut into florets
1 head of red- or green-leaf lettuce, washed and dried
Mustard dressing
2 tbsp. grainy mustard
3 tbsp. balsamic vinegar, or 2½ tbsp. red wine vinegar mixed with 1 tsp. honey
1 tbsp. chopped fresh parsley
2 tsp. chopped fresh oregano, or ½ tsp. dried oregano
freshly ground black pepper
1 tbsp. safflower oil

Preheat the oven to 450° F. Put the mushrooms in a large baking dish. Add the shallots, lemon juice, thyme, salt, some pepper and the tablespoon of oil; toss the mixture to coat the mushrooms. Spread the mushrooms in a single layer, then roast them until they are tender and most of the liquid has evaporated — 20 to 25 minutes. Remove the mushrooms from the oven and keep the dish warm.

While the mushrooms are cooking, make the dressing. Combine the mustard, vinegar, parsley, oregano and some pepper in a small bowl. Whisking vigorously, pour in the tablespoon of oil in a thin, steady stream. Continue whisking until the dressing is well combined; set the dressing aside.

Pour enough water into a saucepan to fill it about 1 inch deep. Set a vegetable steamer in the pan and bring the water to a boil. Put the broccoli florets into the steamer, cover the pan, and steam the broccoli until it is tender but still crisp — about four minutes. Add the broccoli to the dish with the mushrooms. Pour the dressing over the vegetables and toss the salad well. Arrange the salad on a bed of the lettuce leaves; it may be served warm or chilled.

Mango and Grape Salad with Cardamom-Yogurt Dressing

THIS RECIPE CALLS FOR NONFAT DRY MILK, WHICH
SERVES TO THICKEN THE DRESSING.

Serves 8 as a first course or side dish
Working (and total) time: about 50 minutes

Calories **110**
Protein **4g.**
Cholesterol **2mg.**
Total fat **1g.**
Saturated fat **0g.**
Sodium **30mg.**

4 cardamom pods, or ¼ tsp. ground cardamom
1 tsp. finely grated fresh ginger
1 cup plain low-fat yogurt
2 tbsp. fresh orange juice
1 tbsp. honey
2 tbsp. nonfat dry milk

1 head of romaine lettuce, washed and dried
3 firm mangoes, peeled and cut into ½-inch cubes
2 cups halved seedless red or green grapes, or a mixture of both
1 tbsp. coarsely chopped unsalted pistachio nuts

Remove the cardamom seeds from their pods and grind them with a mortar and pestle. Place the ground spice in a bowl and add the ginger, yogurt, orange juice, honey and dry milk. Whisk the ingredients together. Let the dressing stand at room temperature for at least 20 minutes to thicken it and to allow the flavors to meld.

To assemble the salad, arrange the lettuce leaves on individual plates and spoon the mango and grapes onto the lettuce. Pour the dressing over each salad and sprinkle the chopped pistachios on top. Serve at once.

Midsummer Melon Salad with Almond Oil

Serves 6 as a first course or side dish
Working time: about 30 minutes
Total time: about 1 hour and 30 minutes (includes chilling)

Calories **120**
Protein **2g.**
Cholesterol **0mg.**
Total fat **3g.**
Saturated fat **0g.**
Sodium **70mg.**

1 Crenshaw melon, seeded, the flesh cut into 1½-inch-long pieces
½ cantaloupe, seeded, the flesh cut into 1½-inch-long pieces
½ honeydew melon, seeded, the flesh cut into 1½-inch-long pieces
1 tbsp. coarsely chopped fresh ginger
⅛ tsp. salt
freshly ground black pepper
¼ cup rice vinegar
1 tbsp. almond or walnut oil

Combine all the melon pieces in a bowl.

Using a mortar and pestle, crush the chopped fresh ginger with the salt and a generous grinding of pepper. Pour in the rice vinegar and continue crushing to extract as much juice from the ginger as possible. Working over the bowl containing the melon, strain the ginger-vinegar mixture through several layers of cheesecloth: Twist the corners of the cheesecloth in your hands and squeeze hard to extract the last few drops of liquid from the ginger.

Drizzle the almond or walnut oil over the melon pieces and gently toss them to distribute the dressing. Serve the salad well chilled.

Savory Fruit Salad in Red-Wine Jelly

Serves 12 as a side dish
Working time: about 30 minutes
Total time: about 4 hours and 30 minutes
(includes chilling)

Calories **110**
Protein **2g.**
Cholesterol **0mg.**
Total fat **0g.**
Saturated fat **0g.**
Sodium **5mg.**

3 cups red wine
¼ cup sugar
1 tbsp. fresh lemon or lime juice
10 black peppercorns
1 cinnamon stick, broken into pieces
1½ tbsp. unflavored powdered gelatin, softened in 2 tbsp. cold water
2 apricots or 1 peach, pitted and cut into ½-inch pieces
1 firm yellow apple, quartered, cored and cut into ½-inch pieces
2 red plums, pitted and cut into ½-inch pieces
1 cup seedless green grapes, cut in half
1¼ cups Bing cherries, halved and pitted
1 pint strawberries, stemmed and quartered, any very large quarters cut in half
¼ tsp. ground cinnamon
⅛ tsp. ground cloves
freshly ground black pepper

To prepare the wine jelly, first pour the wine into a large, nonreactive saucepan; add the sugar, lemon or lime juice, peppercorns and cinnamon stick. Bring the liquid to a boil, then lower the heat to medium and simmer the mixture until it is reduced by half — about 15 minutes. Strain the liquid through a fine sieve into a large bowl. Add the gelatin to the liquid and stir until the gelatin dissolves. Put the bowl into the refrigerator.

When the wine jelly has cooled and become syrupy, stir in the fruit, ground cinnamon, cloves and a generous grinding of pepper. Pour the salad into a 2-quart mold and chill it until it is firm — about four hours.

To unmold the salad, run the tip of a knife around the inside of the mold to loosen the sides. Briefly dip the bottom of the mold into hot water. Invert a plate on top of the mold, then turn both over together; if necessary, rap the bottom of the mold to free the salad. Lift away the mold and serve the salad at once.

EDITOR'S NOTE: *This salad deliciously complements roast lamb, pork or beef, or grilled chicken breasts.*

Fresh Fruit Salad with Cranberry Dressing

Serves 8 as a side dish
Working time: about 15 minutes
Total time: about 25 minutes

Calories **105**
Protein **1g.**
Cholesterol **0mg.**
Total fat **4g.**
Saturated fat **0g.**
Sodium **40mg.**

½ cup fresh cranberries, or ½ cup frozen cranberries, defrosted
¼ cup white vinegar
1 tbsp. honey
½ tbsp. finely chopped shallot
⅛ tsp. salt
2 tbsp. safflower oil
4 tart red apples, cored and cut into cubes
2 cups seedless green grapes, halved
juice of 1 lemon
1 head of Boston lettuce, or 2 heads of Bibb lettuce, washed and dried

Put the cranberries, vinegar and honey in a small saucepan and bring the mixture to a boil. Reduce the heat to medium low and simmer the mixture until the cranberries are quite soft and the juice has thickened — about five minutes. Purée the mixture in a food processor or blender, then strain it through a fine sieve. Set the cranberry purée aside and allow it to cool to room temperature.

Whisk the shallot, salt and oil into the cooled purée. Toss the apples and grapes with the lemon juice. Arrange the lettuce leaves on eight individual plates and spoon the fruit onto the leaves. Ladle the purée evenly over the salads.

2 An array of staples — pinto beans, black beans, chick-peas, lentils, red lentils, black-eyed peas, rice and pasta — awaits transformation into hearty salads.

A New Life for Old Standbys

Such is the versatility of salad that it need not always be made of fresh greens or fruit to find an important place in a meal. Lentils, chick-peas and dried beans, white and brown rice, cracked wheat and barley, wild rice, and pasta — all these and more are the foundation for the 28 appetizing and highly nutritious salads that make up this section.

They have in common their chameleon-like ability to adapt — a quality that serves them well in salads, where they can take on the tastes and aromas of the ingredients with which they are combined.

Among other contributions grains and dried beans make to a salad is texture, whether chewy in the case of wild rice, or pleasantly mealy in the case of beans. To ensure that they preserve their texture, all require careful cooking. A processed grain such as bulgur (wheat that has previously been steamed, cracked and dried) has only to be soaked in water for a relatively brief period to make it edible. Whole grains — barley, wheat berries, millet and the like — demand longer cooking. Brown rice, which has a tough outer coating, takes twice as long to cook as white rice — 35 minutes or more. Dried beans, instead of having to be soaked overnight to soften them, can be prepared in less time by bringing them to a quick boil, then allowing them to soak for one hour before simmering them in a change of water for one to two hours. Pasta should be cooked until it is *al dente,* drained and rinsed in cold running water to prevent it from sticking together.

Salads made of grains, dried beans and pasta will obviously be quite a bit more filling than those concocted of greens, and thus some may serve as main courses. Not the least of their attractions is that they can all be prepared in advance — and will often be better when they are, since their flavors then have a chance to develop and mellow.

Brown Rice and Mango Salad

Serves 8 as a side dish
Working time: about 20 minutes
Total time: about 1 hour and 30 minutes

Calories **140**
Protein **2g.**
Cholesterol **0mg.**
Total fat **4g.**
Saturated fat **0g.**
Sodium **70mg.**

1 cup brown rice
¼ cup red wine vinegar
¼ tsp. salt
2 tbsp. safflower oil
1 cubanelle or other mild green pepper, seeded and diced
1 small shallot, finely chopped
⅛ tsp. ground cardamom
mace
cayenne pepper
1 ripe mango, peeled and diced

Bring 6 cups of water to a boil in a large saucepan. Stir in the rice, reduce the heat and simmer the rice, uncovered, until it is tender — about 35 minutes. Drain the rice and put it in a serving bowl. Stir in the vinegar and salt, and allow the mixture to cool to room temperature — about 30 minutes.

When the rice is cool, stir in the oil, pepper, shallot, cardamom and a pinch each of mace and cayenne pepper. Add the mango pieces and stir them in gently so that they retain their shape. Cover the salad; to allow the flavors to meld, let the salad stand, unrefrigerated, for about 30 minutes before serving it.

Kasha with Wild Mushrooms and Peas

Serves 6 as a side dish
Working (and total) time: about 45 minutes

Calories **110**
Protein **4g.**
Cholesterol **0mg.**
Total fat **3g.**
Saturated fat **0g.**
Sodium **90mg.**

¼ oz. dried wild mushrooms
1½ lb. fresh green peas, shelled, or 1½ cups frozen peas, defrosted
1 cup kasha (cracked buckwheat groats)
½ lb. fresh mushrooms, wiped clean, stems trimmed
¼ cup fresh lemon juice
1 tbsp. balsamic vinegar, or ¾ tbsp. red wine vinegar mixed with ¼ tsp. honey
1 small shallot, finely chopped
¼ tsp. salt
freshly ground black pepper
1 tbsp. safflower oil

Soak the dried mushrooms in 1 cup of very hot water for 20 minutes, then drain them, reserving their soaking liquid. Chop the mushrooms and set them aside.

If you are using fresh peas, boil them until they are tender — five to seven minutes. (Frozen peas do not require boiling.) Drain the peas and set them aside.

While the mushrooms are soaking, add the kasha to 2 cups of boiling water and cook it, stirring frequently, until it is tender — about five minutes. Drain the kasha, rinse it well, and drain it again. Transfer the kasha to a large bowl.

Slice the fresh mushrooms and put them into a small bowl with the lemon juice; the juice will prevent them from discoloring. Toss the mushrooms well and set the bowl aside.

To prepare the dressing, strain the reserved soaking liquid through a cheesecloth-lined sieve into a small saucepan. Cook the liquid over medium-high heat until only about 2 tablespoons remain — approximately five minutes. Pour the liquid into a small bowl; add the lemon juice from the bowl containing the fresh mushrooms, then add the vinegar, shallot, salt and some pepper. Stir the ingredients together. Whisking vigorously, pour in the oil in a thin, steady stream. Continue whisking until the dressing is well combined. Set the dressing aside.

Add to the kasha the peas, the dried and fresh mushrooms, and the dressing. Combine the ingredients well and serve the salad at once.

Millet Tabbouleh

TABBOULEH, A MIDDLE EASTERN SALAD, IS TRADITIONALLY
MADE WITH BULGUR. HERE MILLET PROVIDES A NEW TOUCH.

Serves 6 as a side dish
Working time: about 15 minutes
Total time: about 1 hour (includes chilling)

Calories **160**
Protein **4g.**
Cholesterol **0mg.**
Total fat **4g.**
Saturated fat **0g.**
Sodium **80mg.**

1 cup millet
⅛ tsp. salt
freshly ground black pepper
⅓ cup raisins
3 cups loosely packed stemmed parsley sprigs
1 shallot, finely chopped
2 tbsp. finely chopped cilantro
2 tbsp. fresh lemon juice
2 tsp. honey
2 tsp. Dijon mustard
1 tbsp. safflower oil
1 head of Boston lettuce, or 2 heads of Bibb lettuce, washed and dried

Pour 2 cups of water into a saucepan and bring it to a simmer over medium heat. Stir in the millet, salt and a generous grinding of pepper. Cover the pan and cook the millet until the water level drops just below the surface of the millet — 10 to 15 minutes. Stir in the raisins and reduce the heat to low; continue cooking the millet, covered, until all the water has been absorbed — about seven minutes more.

Transfer the contents of the pan to a large bowl. Immediately stir in the parsley sprigs; the hot millet will cook them slightly. Loosely cover the bowl with plastic wrap and allow the millet to cool.

Meanwhile, combine the shallot, cilantro, lemon juice, honey and mustard in a small bowl. Whisk in the oil. When the millet has cooled to room temperature, pour the dressing over it and toss the salad well. Serve chilled with the lettuce.

Polenta Salad with Ham

Serves 6 as a first course or side dish
Working time: about 40 minutes
Total time: about 50 minutes

Calories **140**
Protein **4g.**
Cholesterol **5mg.**
Total fat **4g.**
Saturated fat **1g.**
Sodium **220mg.**

¼ tsp. salt
1 tsp. dried oregano, or 1 tbsp. chopped fresh oregano
1 cup stone-ground cornmeal
1 tbsp. virgin olive oil
3 scallions, trimmed and sliced, the white parts kept separate from the green
2 ripe tomatoes (about 1 lb.), peeled, seeded and chopped
¼ cup red wine vinegar
freshly ground black pepper
1 slice of ham (about 2 oz.), diced

Bring 2¼ cups of water to a boil in a large saucepan with ⅛ teaspoon of the salt and half of the oregano.

Sprinkle in the cornmeal, stirring continuously with a wooden spoon. Reduce the heat to medium and cook the polenta, stirring constantly, until all the liquid has been absorbed and the polenta is quite stiff — 10 to 15 minutes. Spoon the polenta onto a large, lightly oiled plate and spread it out to a uniform thickness of about ½ inch. Refrigerate the polenta uncovered while you prepare the dressing. Preheat the oven to 350° F.

Heat the oil in a heavy-bottomed skillet over medium heat. Add the white scallion parts and the remaining oregano, and cook them for one minute. Stir in the tomatoes, vinegar, the remaining ⅛ teaspoon of salt and some pepper. Cook the mixture, stirring occasionally, for 15 minutes. Transfer the contents of the pan to a blender or food processor, and purée the mixture until a smooth dressing results. Pour the dressing into a large bowl and chill it while you finish the salad.

Cut the polenta into strips about ½ inch wide and 1½ inches long. Transfer the strips to a lightly oiled baking sheet and bake them for 10 minutes to dry them out, turning them occasionally with a metal spatula. Immediately transfer the strips to the bowl with the dressing. Add the green scallion parts, the ham and a generous grinding of pepper. Toss the salad well and serve it without delay.

Apricots and Water Chestnuts in Wild Rice

Serves 8 as a side dish
Working time: about 30 minutes
Total time: about 1 hour

Calories **130**
Protein **4g.**
Cholesterol **0mg.**
Total fat **0g.**
Saturated fat **0g.**
Sodium **75mg.**

1 cup wild rice
¼ lb. dried apricots, cut into ½-inch pieces
6 oz. fresh water chestnuts, peeled and quartered, or one 8 oz. can whole peeled water chestnuts, drained, rinsed and quartered
2 tbsp. chopped fresh parsley
Spicy lemon dressing
2 tbsp. fresh lemon juice
1 tbsp. red wine vinegar
⅛ tsp. ground ginger
⅛ tsp. cinnamon
ground cloves
¼ tsp. salt
freshly ground black pepper

Bring 6 cups of water to a boil in a saucepan. Stir in the wild rice, reduce the heat, and simmer the rice, uncovered, until it is tender but still chewy — approximately 45 minutes.

While the rice cooks, prepare the apricots and dressing: Put the apricots into a small bowl and pour in enough hot water to cover them by about 1 inch. Soak the apricots for 20 minutes to soften them. Drain the apricots, reserving ¼ cup of their soaking liquid, and set them aside.

Pour the reserved apricot-soaking liquid into a small bowl. Add the lemon juice, vinegar, ginger, cinnamon, a pinch of cloves, the salt and some pepper; whisk the mixture vigorously until it is thoroughly combined.

When the rice finishes cooking, drain and rinse it and transfer it to a serving bowl. Pour the dressing over the rice, then add the apricots, water chestnuts and the parsley; toss the ingredients well and serve the salad at room temperature.

Saffron Rice Salad with Peppers and Chick-Peas

Serves 12 as a side dish
Working time: about 30 minutes
Total time: about 2 hours and 45 minutes

Calories **180**
Protein **5g.**
Cholesterol **0mg.**
Total fat **7g.**
Saturated fat **1g.**
Sodium **145mg.**

⅔ cup dried chick-peas, picked over
¼ tsp. salt
1½ cups long-grain rice
2½ cups unsalted chicken stock or water
½ tsp. saffron threads, soaked for 10 minutes in ¼ cup very hot water
1 lemon-zest strip
1 lb. fresh green peas, shelled, or 1 cup frozen green peas, defrosted
¼ cup whole unskinned almonds
1 sweet red pepper, seeded, deribbed and cut into thin slices
1 green pepper, seeded, deribbed and cut into thin slices
2 ripe tomatoes, seeded and chopped
6 oil-cured black olives, thinly sliced
⅓ cup vinaigrette (recipe, page 13)

Rinse the chick-peas under cold running water. Put the chick-peas in a large, heavy-bottomed pot and pour in enough cold water to cover them by about 2 inches. Discard any chick-peas that float to the surface. Cover the pot, leaving the lid ajar, and bring the water to a boil; cook the chick-peas for two minutes. Turn off the heat, cover the pot, and soak the peas for at least an hour. (Alternatively, soak the chick-peas overnight in cold water.)

When the chick-peas finish soaking, drain them well in a colander. Return them to the pot and pour in enough water to cover them by about 2 inches. Bring the liquid to a simmer; cook the chick-peas over medium-low heat until they are soft — about 45 minutes. Stir in the salt and continue cooking the chick-peas until they are quite tender — 10 to 15 minutes more. (If the chick-peas appear to be drying out at any point, pour in more water.)

About 20 minutes before the chick-peas finish cooking, start the rice: Bring the stock or water to a boil in a saucepan, then add the rice, the saffron and its soaking liquid, and the lemon zest. Stir the rice to distribute the saffron and return the liquid to a boil. Cover the pan and cook the rice over medium-low heat until it is tender and has absorbed all the liquid — about 20 minutes. Discard the lemon zest.

While the rice is cooking, boil the fresh peas until ▶

they are tender — five to seven minutes. Drain the peas and set them aside. (Frozen peas do not require boiling.) Heat the almonds in a small, heavy-bottomed skillet over medium heat, stirring them frequently until they are lightly toasted — about five minutes.

Drain the chick-peas well and transfer them to a large bowl. Add the rice, green peas, toasted almonds, red and green peppers, tomatoes and olives. Pour the prepared vinaigrette over the salad and toss the ingredients well to coat them. Transfer the salad to a serving dish. Serve at room temperature or barely chilled.

Calories **280**
Protein **6g.**
Cholesterol **0mg.**
Total fat **5g.**
Saturated fat **1g.**
Sodium **125mg.**

Wheat Berry and Orange Salad

Serves 6 as a first course or side dish
Working time: about 45 minutes
Total time: about 2 hours

1 cup wheat berries
¼ tsp. salt
6 Valencia or navel oranges (about ½ lb. each)
½ cup raisins
2 tsp. sherry vinegar or red wine vinegar
1 tbsp. grainy mustard
2 tbsp. virgin olive oil
freshly ground black pepper
1 tsp. grated orange zest
½ cup thinly sliced scallion
¼ cup thinly sliced mint leaves
6 mint sprigs for garnish

Bring 2 cups of water to a boil in a saucepan. Stir in the wheat berries and salt. Reduce the heat to low, cover the pan, and simmer the kernels until they are tender — one and a half to two hours. If the wheat berries absorb all the water before they finish cooking, pour in more water, ¼ cup at a time, to keep the kernels from burning. Drain the wheat berries and set them aside to cool.

While the wheat berries are cooking, hollow out the oranges as shown. Using your fingers, a knife or a spoon, separate ½ cup of the orange flesh from the pulp; coarsely chop the flesh and set it aside. Squeeze the juice from the remaining pulp and reserve ½ cup of it. (Save the rest of the juice for another use.) Combine the ½ cup of juice in a small bowl with the raisins; let the raisins soak for 15 minutes.

To prepare the dressing, transfer 2 tablespoons of the raisin-soaking liquid to a large bowl. Add the vinegar and mustard. Slowly whisk in the oil, then season the dressing with some pepper.

Add to the bowl the drained wheat berries, chopped orange flesh, orange zest, raisins with their remaining soaking liquid, scallion and sliced mint. Stir to combine the ingredients, then spoon the mixture into the orange shells. Replace the orange tops and garnish each shell with a sprig of mint before serving.

How to Make an Orange Cup

1 *REMOVING THE TOP. With a boning knife, as here, or a paring knife, slice off the top of an orange about 1 inch from the stem end. Reserve the top to use later as a cover for the cup; to prevent drying, place the top flesh side down on a plate.*

2 *CUTTING AROUND THE CORE. Holding the orange at an angle, insert the knife tip between the flesh and the rind, and dig deep into the fruit. With a gentle sawing motion, cut around the rim to separate as much of the flesh from the rind as possible.*

3 *EXTRACTING THE FLESH. Hold the orange over a bowl to catch the juice, and insert a sturdy soupspoon into the cut. Dig around the cut with the spoon, while rotating the orange in your other hand. Scoop out the core.*

4 *EMPTYING THE SHELL. Grasping the spoon firmly, dig under the membrane to remove the residual pulp and juice. Thoroughly scrape the interior to bare the white wall.*

Bulgur Salad with Raisins and Zucchini

Serves 12 as a side dish
Working time: about 20 minutes
Total time: about 1 hour and 30 minutes
(includes soaking and chilling)

Calories **125**
Protein **4g.**
Cholesterol **0mg.**
Total fat **1g.**
Saturated fat **0g.**
Sodium **5mg.**

2 cups bulgur
2 zucchini, each cut crosswise into ¼-inch slices, each slice cut into eight wedges
5 scallions, trimmed and sliced
½ cup red wine vinegar
1 yellow pepper, seeded, deribbed and cut into ½-inch squares
¼ cup raisins
⅛ tsp. cayenne pepper
⅛ tsp. ground cardamom
⅛ tsp. ground coriander
ground cloves
ground ginger
ground mace

Put the bulgur into a heatproof bowl and pour 3 cups of boiling water over it. Cover the bowl and set it aside for 30 minutes.

At the end of the soaking period, mix in the zucchini, scallions, vinegar, yellow pepper, raisins, cayenne pepper, cardamom, coriander, and a pinch each of cloves, ginger and mace. Let the salad stand for at least 30 minutes before serving it either chilled or at room temperature.

Chick-Pea Purée on Romaine Lettuce Leaves

Serves 8 as a first course or side dish
Working time: about 45 minutes
Total time: about 3 hours (includes soaking)

Calories **70**
Protein **5g.**
Cholesterol **2mg.**
Total fat **3g.**
Saturated fat **0g.**
Sodium **60mg.**

1 cup dried chick-peas, picked over
1 garlic clove, quartered
¼ cup celery leaves
¼ cup freshly grated Parmesan cheese
2 tbsp. pine nuts
¼ cup fresh lemon juice
⅛ tsp. white pepper
2 heads of romaine lettuce, washed and dried
1 small ripe tomato, chopped
2 tbsp. chopped red onion
2 tbsp. chopped green pepper (optional)

Rinse the chick-peas under cold running water, then transfer them to a large pot and pour in enough water to cover them by about 2 inches. Discard any chick-peas that float to the surface. Cover the pot, leaving the lid ajar, and bring the liquid to a boil; cook the peas for two minutes. Turn off the heat, cover the pot, and soak the peas for at least an hour. (Alternatively, soak the peas overnight in cold water.)

At the end of the soaking period, drain the chick-peas and return them to the pot with 3 cups of water. Bring the liquid to a strong simmer, then reduce the heat to medium low, and cook the peas, covered, until they are quite tender — about one hour and 15 minutes. (If the peas appear to be drying out at any point, pour in more water, a cup at a time.)

Drain the chick-peas, catching their cooking liquid in a bowl. Set the bowl aside. Press the chick-peas through a sieve, then put them in a blender or food processor with the garlic, celery leaves, Parmesan cheese, pine nuts, 3 tablespoons of the lemon juice and the white pepper. With the motor running, pour in 1 cup of the reserved cooking liquid in a slow, thin stream — a smooth paste should result. If need be, incorporate as much as ½ cup of additional cooking liquid. (Unsalted chicken stock or water may be used to augment the cooking liquid.)

Remove the outer lettuce leaves and reserve them for another use. Spread about 1 tablespoon of the chick-pea purée over the stem end of each inner leaf. Mound the remaining purée in the middle of a serving plate and arrange the leaves around it. Chill the salad for at least 20 minutes. Just before serving, garnish the salad with the tomato, the onion and the green pepper if you are using it; drizzle the remaining tablespoon of lemon juice over the top of the purée.

Black Bean, Rice and Pepper Salad

Serves 4 as a main course
Working time: about 20 minutes
Total time: about 4 hours (includes soaking and chilling)

Calories **635**
Protein **21g.**
Cholesterol **2mg.**
Total fat **10g.**
Saturated fat **1g.**
Sodium **385mg.**

1 cup black beans, picked over
1 small onion, coarsely chopped
1 garlic clove
2 tsp. fresh thyme, or ½ tsp. dried thyme leaves
1 bay leaf
½ tsp. salt
4 cups unsalted chicken stock
2 cups rice
2 shallots, finely chopped
1 sweet red pepper, seeded, deribbed and sliced into short, thin strips
1 green pepper, seeded, deribbed and sliced into short, thin strips
1 jalapeño pepper, seeded and finely chopped (caution, page 17)
3 scallions, trimmed and thinly sliced
2 tbsp. chopped cilantro or parsley

Chili dressing

1 tsp. Dijon mustard
1 tbsp. sherry vinegar or white wine vinegar
1 tbsp. unsalted chicken stock
2 tbsp. virgin olive oil
½ tsp. chili powder
4 drops hot red-pepper sauce
1 garlic clove, finely chopped
freshly ground black pepper

Rinse the beans under cold running water, then put them into a large, heavy-bottomed pot, and pour in enough cold water to cover them by about 3 inches.

Discard any beans that float to the surface. Cover the pot, leaving the lid ajar, and slowly bring the water to a boil. Cook the beans for two minutes. Then turn off the heat, cover the pot, and soak the beans for at least an hour. (Alternatively, soak the beans overnight in cold water.)

Add the onion, garlic, thyme and bay leaf to the beans; bring the beans to a simmer over medium-low heat and tightly cover the pot. Cook the beans, occasionally skimming foam from the surface of the liquid, until they are soft — about one hour. Stir in the salt and continue cooking the beans until they are quite tender — 30 minutes to one hour more. If the beans appear to be drying out at any point, pour in more water.

Transfer the cooked beans to a colander. Remove the garlic clove and bay leaf, then rinse the beans, and drain them well.

Bring the stock to a boil in a small saucepan. Add the rice and shallots, and lower the heat to maintain a simmer. Cook the rice, covered, until it is tender and the liquid is absorbed — about 20 minutes.

While the rice is cooking, prepare the dressing. Combine the mustard, vinegar and the tablespoon of stock in a small bowl. Whisk in the oil, then the chili powder, red-pepper sauce, garlic and some pepper.

Transfer the hot rice to a large bowl. Add the peppers, scallions and beans. Pour the dressing over the salad, toss well, and chill the salad for at least one hour. Sprinkle the salad with the cilantro or parsley just before serving.

Red Lentils with White Rice and Pearl Onions

Serves 6 as a side dish
Working time: about 15 minutes
Total time: about 30 minutes

Calories **200**
Protein **8g.**
Cholesterol **0mg.**
Total fat **3g.**
Saturated fat **0g.**
Sodium **20mg.**

1 cup red lentils, picked over
½ cup rice
2 tbsp. sugar
4 tbsp. raspberry vinegar
6 tbsp. unsalted chicken stock
1½ cups pearl onions, blanched for 2 minutes in boiling water and peeled
1 tsp. Dijon mustard
freshly ground black pepper
1 tbsp. safflower oil

Bring the lentils and 3 cups of water to a boil in a small saucepan over medium-high heat. Reduce the heat and simmer the lentils until they are tender — 15 to 20 minutes. Avoid overcooking or the lentils will lose much of their color. Drain the lentils and put them into a large bowl.

Start cooking the rice while the lentils are simmering. Bring the rice and 1 cup of water to a boil in a small saucepan over medium-high heat. Reduce the heat, cover the saucepan, and simmer the rice until the liquid has been absorbed and the rice is tender — about 20 minutes. Add the rice to the lentils.

While the rice is cooking, sprinkle the sugar into a skillet and set it over medium heat. Cook the sugar until it liquifies and starts to caramelize. Pour in 3 tablespoons of the vinegar and 4 tablespoons of the chicken stock. As the liquid comes to a simmer, stir it to incorporate the caramelized sugar, then add the pearl onions. Cook the onions, stirring from time to time, until they are glazed and nearly all the liquid in the skillet has evaporated. Add the onions to the lentils and rice.

To prepare the dressing, combine the remaining tablespoon of raspberry vinegar and 2 tablespoons of chicken stock, the mustard and some pepper in a small bowl. Whisk in the oil, then pour the vinaigrette over the lentil-and-rice mixture, and toss well. This salad is best served cold.

Eggplant, Cucumber and White Bean Salad

Serves 12 as a side dish
Working time: about 30 minutes
Total time: about 3 hours (includes soaking and chilling)

Calories **120**
Protein **7g.**
Cholesterol **0mg.**
Total fat **1g.**
Saturated fat **0g.**
Sodium **95mg.**

1 lb. navy beans, picked over
¾ lb. eggplant, cut into ½-inch cubes
1 onion, chopped
½ tsp. sugar
¼ cup raspberry vinegar or red wine vinegar
1 tsp. chopped fresh sage, or ¼ tsp. dried sage, crushed
1 garlic clove, finely chopped
½ tsp. salt
freshly ground black pepper
1 hydroponic cucumber, cut into ½-inch cubes, or 2 regular cucumbers, peeled, seeded and cut into ½-inch cubes

Rinse the beans under cold running water, then put them into a large, heavy pot, and pour in enough cold water to cover them by about 3 inches. Discard any beans that float to the surface. Cover the pot, leaving the lid ajar, and slowly bring the liquid to a boil. Boil the beans for two minutes, then turn off the heat, and soak the beans, covered, for at least an hour. (Alternatively, soak the beans overnight in cold water.)

Preheat the oven to 500° F.

If the beans have absorbed all of their soaking liquid, pour in enough water to cover them again by about 3 inches. Bring the liquid to a boil, reduce the heat to maintain a strong simmer, and cook the beans until they are tender — about one hour.

While the beans are cooking, put the eggplant cubes into a lightly oiled baking dish and bake them until they are a golden brown — about 20 minutes. Meanwhile, combine the onion with the sugar and 2 tablespoons of the vinegar; set the mixture aside. When the eggplant cubes are browned, transfer them to a bowl; toss the cubes with the remaining 2 tablespoons of vinegar and set the bowl aside until the beans finish cooking.

Drain the cooked beans and rinse them under cold running water. Combine them with the marinated eggplant and onion. Add the sage, garlic, salt, some pepper and the cucumber, and mix well. Serve the salad at room temperature or chill it for at least 30 minutes before serving.

Red and White Bean Salad

Serves 8 as a first course or side dish
Working time: about 25 minutes
Total time: about 2 hours and 20 minutes
(includes soaking)

Calories **200**
Protein **11g.**
Cholesterol **0mg.**
Total fat **3g.**
Saturated fat **0g.**
Sodium **95mg.**

½ lb. red kidney beans, picked over
½ lb. Great Northern beans, picked over
1 small celeriac
1 small onion, thinly sliced
2 tsp. finely chopped fresh ginger
¼ cup red wine vinegar
¼ tsp. salt
freshly ground black pepper
1 tbsp. chopped cilantro
1 large, ripe tomato, chopped
1½ tbsp. safflower oil

Rinse the kidney beans under cold running water, then put them into a large pot with enough cold water to cover them by about 3 inches. Rinse the Great Northern beans and put them in a separate pot; pour in enough cold water to cover them by about 3 inches. Discard any beans that float to the surface. Cover the pots, leaving the lids ajar, and slowly bring the liquid in each one to a boil. Boil the beans for two minutes, then turn off the heat, and soak the beans, covered, for at least an hour. (Alternatively, soak the beans overnight in cold water.)

If the beans absorb all of their soaking liquid, add enough water to cover them again by 3 inches. Bring the liquid in each pot to a boil, reduce the heat to maintain a strong simmer, and cook the beans until they are just tender — 50 to 60 minutes.

While the beans are cooking, peel the celeriac and cut it into ½-inch cubes. Transfer the cubes to a salad bowl and toss them with the onion, ginger and vinegar. Set the bowl aside at room temperature.

Drain the cooked beans and rinse them under cold running water. Drain the beans again and add them to the bowl along with the salt, some pepper, the cilantro, tomato and oil; mix well, and serve chilled or at room temperature.

Lentil and Mushroom Salad

Serves 6 as a side dish
Working time: about 40 minutes
Total time: about 1 hour and 40 minutes
(includes chilling)

Calories **165**
Protein **8g.**
Cholesterol **0mg.**
Total fat **5g.**
Saturated fat **1g.**
Sodium **165mg.**

¾ cup lentils, picked over
1 small onion, studded with 4 whole cloves
1 bay leaf
2 tsp. fresh thyme, or ½ tsp. dried thyme leaves
3 carrots, thinly sliced
3 celery stalks, sliced
3 scallions, trimmed and thinly sliced
6 oz. mushrooms, wiped clean, trimmed and thinly sliced
2 tbsp. fresh lemon juice
3 or 4 leaves romaine lettuce, cut into chiffonade (technique, page 51)
2 ripe tomatoes, each cut into 8 wedges
1 tbsp. chopped parsley

Spicy mustard vinaigrette
1 tbsp. Dijon mustard
2 tbsp. fresh lemon juice
2 tsp. hot red-pepper sauce
2 garlic cloves, finely chopped
¼ tsp. salt
freshly ground black pepper
2 tbsp. virgin olive oil

Rinse the lentils and put them into a saucepan with 4 cups of water. Add the onion, bay leaf and thyme, and bring the water to a boil. Reduce the heat to maintain a simmer and cook the lentils until they are tender — about 25 minutes. Drain the lentils, discard the onion and the bay leaf, and transfer the lentils to a large bowl. Add the carrots, celery and scallions, and toss the mixture well.

Put the mushrooms and the lemon juice into a

saucepan; pour in enough water to just cover the mushrooms, and bring the water to a boil. Cover the pan, reduce the heat, and simmer the mushrooms until they are tender — about five minutes. Drain the mushrooms and add them to the bowl containing the other vegetables.

To prepare the vinaigrette, whisk together the mustard, lemon juice, hot red-pepper sauce, garlic, salt, some pepper and the oil. Pour the vinaigrette over the lentil mixture, toss well, and refrigerate it for at least one hour.

To serve the salad, mound the lentil mixture in the center of a serving plate and arrange the lettuce around the lentil salad. Garnish with the tomato wedges and sprinkle the chopped parsley over all.

Curried Black-Eyed Peas

Serves 6 as a side dish
Working time: about 20 minutes
Total time: about 2 hours and 30 minutes
(includes soaking and chilling)

Calories **105**
Protein **5g.**
Cholesterol **0mg.**
Total fat **3g.**
Saturated fat **0g.**
Sodium **100mg.**

1 cup dried black-eyed peas, picked over
¼ tsp. salt
½ cup unsalted chicken stock
2 bunches scallions, trimmed and cut into 1-inch lengths
1½ tbsp. fresh lemon juice
1 tbsp. red wine vinegar or white wine vinegar
½ tbsp. honey
1¼ tsp. curry powder
freshly ground black pepper
1 tbsp. virgin olive oil
½ sweet red pepper, seeded, deribbed and cut into bâtonnets

Rinse the black-eyed peas under cold running water, then put them into a large saucepan, and pour in enough cold water to cover them by about 3 inches. Discard any peas that float to the surface. Bring the water to a boil and cook the peas for two minutes. Turn off the heat, partially cover the pot, and soak the peas for at least an hour. (Alternatively, soak the peas overnight in cold water.)

Bring the peas to a simmer over medium-low heat and tightly cover the pot. Cook the peas, occasionally skimming any foam from the surface of the liquid, until they begin to soften — about 45 minutes. Stir in the salt and continue cooking the peas until they are quite tender — about 15 minutes more. If the peas appear to be drying out at any point, pour in more water.

While the peas are cooking, heat the stock in a large skillet over medium heat. Add the scallions and partially cover the skillet. Cook the scallions, stirring often, until almost all the liquid has evaporated — eight to 10 minutes. Transfer the contents of the skillet to a bowl.

In a smaller bowl, combine the lemon juice, vinegar, honey, curry powder and some pepper. Whisk in the oil and set the dressing aside.

Transfer the cooked peas to a colander; rinse and drain them. Add the peas and the red pepper to the scallions in the bowl. Pour the dressing over all and toss the salad well. Chill the salad for at least 30 minutes before serving.

Lentil Salad
with Sweet Red Peppers

Serves 12 as a side dish
Working time: about 1 hour
Total time: about 3 hours (includes chilling)

Calories **130**	
Protein **6g.**	
Cholesterol **11mg.**	
Total fat **5g.**	
Saturated fat **1g.**	
Sodium **140mg.**	

1½ cups dried lentils, picked over and rinsed	3 tbsp. very finely chopped fresh chervil (optional)
¼ cup finely chopped fresh tarragon, or 2 tbsp. dried tarragon	¾ tsp. salt
¼ cup tarragon vinegar	freshly ground black pepper
3 sweet red peppers	1 hard-boiled egg
¼ cup virgin olive oil	1 cucumber, preferably unwaxed
8 large garlic cloves	2 or 3 small ripe tomatoes, sliced
¾ cup fresh lemon juice	
¼ cup finely sliced chives or scallions	

Put the lentils in a large, heavy-bottomed pot with 3 cups of water. Bring the water to a boil, then reduce the heat to medium and simmer the lentils until they are tender — about 20 minutes.

If you are using dried tarragon, combine it with the vinegar in a small, nonreactive pan set over medium heat. Bring the liquid to a simmer, then remove the pan from the heat and allow the tarragon to steep for at least 10 minutes.

While the lentils are cooking, roast the peppers about 2 inches below a preheated broiler, turning them until they are blistered on all sides. Place the peppers in a bowl and cover it with plastic wrap; the trapped steam will loosen their skins. Peel and seed the peppers, then finely chop them; set the chopped peppers aside.

Drain the lentils and transfer them to a large bowl. Combine the oil and vinegar in a small bowl and pour the liquid over the lentils. Add the chopped peppers and stir the mixture well, then refrigerate it.

Preheat the oven to 500° F. Place the garlic cloves in a small, ovenproof dish and bake them until they are soft — seven to 10 minutes. When the cloves are cool enough to handle, peel them and press them through a sieve set over a bowl. Whisk the lemon juice into the garlic purée, then stir the purée into the lentil-pepper mixture. Add the chives or scallions, the fresh tarragon and chervil if you are using them, the salt and some pepper; stir well to combine all the ingredients. Refrigerate the salad for at least two hours before serving it.

At serving time, peel the egg and separate the yolk from the white. Press the yolk through a sieve set over a small bowl. Sieve the egg white the same way. Mound the salad on a serving plate; sprinkle half of the egg white and then half of the yolk over the top. (Of course, the whole egg may be used, but doing so will raise the cholesterol level above our guidelines for a side dish.) Cutting the length of the cucumber with a vegetable peeler, pare off alternating strips of skin to achieve a striped effect. Thinly slice the cucumber. Garnish the salad with the sliced cucumber and tomatoes.

EDITOR'S NOTE: *The flavor of this salad will be even better a day later. If you prepare the salad in advance, store it in the refrigerator; do not add the garnishes until serving time.*

Chick-Pea Salad with Cucumber and Dill Sauce

Serves 6 as a side dish
Working time: about 25 minutes
Total time: about 2 hours and 30 minutes
(includes soaking)

Calories **80**
Protein **5g.**
Cholesterol **3mg.**
Total fat **2g.**
Saturated fat **1g.**
Sodium **115mg.**

1 cup dried chick-peas, picked over
2 hydroponic cucumbers, or 4 regular cucumbers, peeled
1 large tomato, peeled, seeded and coarsely chopped
¼ cup finely cut fresh dill
½ cup plain low-fat yogurt
2 tbsp. sour cream
¼ tsp. salt
freshly ground black pepper

Rinse the chick-peas under cold running water, then put them in a large, heavy pot and pour in enough cold water to cover them by about 3 inches. Discard any that float to the surface. Cover the pot, leaving the lid ajar, and slowly bring the liquid to a boil over medium-low heat. Boil the chick-peas for two minutes, then turn off the heat and soak them for at least one hour. (Alternatively, soak the peas overnight in cold water.) If they absorb all the liquid, add enough water to cover them again by about 3 inches. Bring the liquid to a boil, reduce the heat to maintain a strong simmer, and cook the peas until they are tender — about one hour. Drain the peas, rinse them under cold running water, and transfer them to a salad bowl.

Cut one half of one of the hydroponic cucumbers or one of the regular cucumbers into thin slices and set the slices aside. Peel the remaining cucumbers and seed them. Finely chop their flesh and place it on a large square of doubled cheesecloth. Gather the ends and twist them to wring out as much moisture as possible from the cucumbers. Discard the juice.

Combine the chopped cucumber, tomato, dill, yogurt, sour cream, salt and some pepper with the chick-peas, and gently toss the mixture. Serve the salad garnished with the reserved cucumber slices.

Couscous Salad with Snow Peas and Wild Mushrooms

Serves 6 as a first course or side dish
Working time: about 20 minutes
Total time: about 35 minutes

Calories **135**
Protein **5g.**
Cholesterol **0mg.**
Total fat **4g.**
Saturated fat **1g.**
Sodium **150mg.**

1½ cups unsalted chicken stock
¼ cup chopped shallot
2½ tbsp. fresh lemon juice
freshly ground black pepper
1 cup couscous
⅓ cup coarsely chopped cilantro
1½ tbsp. virgin olive oil
¼ lb. fresh cepes, chanterelles or other wild mushrooms, wiped clean and sliced
1 tsp. fresh thyme, or ¼ tsp. dried thyme leaves
¼ lb. snow peas, stems and strings removed, each cut diagonally into 3 pieces
¼ tsp. salt
1 tsp. red wine vinegar
1 head of oakleaf lettuce or red-leaf lettuce, washed and dried

Pour the stock into a large saucepan; add 2 tablespoons of the shallot, 2 tablespoons of the lemon juice and some pepper. Bring the stock to a boil, then stir in the couscous and half of the cilantro. Cover the pan tightly and remove it from the heat; let it stand while you complete the salad.

Meanwhile, heat 1 tablespoon of the oil in a large, heavy-bottomed skillet over medium-high heat. When the oil is hot, add the mushrooms, thyme and the remaining 2 tablespoons of shallot. Sauté the mushrooms until they begin to brown — about four minutes. Stir in the snow peas, the salt and some pepper. Cook the mixture, stirring frequently, for two minutes more. Remove the skillet from the heat.

Transfer the couscous to a large bowl and fluff it with a fork. In a small bowl, combine the vinegar, the remaining ½ tablespoon of oil, the remaining ½ tablespoon of lemon juice and the remaining cilantro. Drizzle this vinaigrette over the couscous and fluff the couscous once again to distribute the dressing evenly. Add the contents of the skillet to the bowl, using a rubber spatula to scrape out the flavor-rich juices. Toss the salad well and chill it for at least 15 minutes.

To serve, arrange the lettuce on a serving platter and mound the salad atop the leaves.

Chilled Spinach Spirals with Shrimp, Eggplant and Yellow Squash

Serves 6 as a main course
Working time: about 35 minutes
Total time: about 45 minutes

Calories **260**
Protein **16g.**
Cholesterol **79mg.**
Total fat **6g.**
Saturated fat **1g.**
Sodium **250mg.**

2 tbsp. virgin olive oil
2½ tbsp. fresh lime juice
1 medium eggplant (about 6 oz.), halved lengthwise, the halves cut crosswise into ½-inch-thick slices
½ lb. spinach rotini (corkscrew pasta) or other fancy spinach pasta
2 ripe plum tomatoes (about ½ lb.)
1 large yellow squash (about ¼ lb.), halved lengthwise, the halves cut diagonally into ½-inch-thick slices
2 shallots, finely chopped
¾ lb. medium shrimp, peeled, and deveined if necessary
1 tsp. fresh thyme, or ¼ tsp. dried thyme leaves
¼ tsp. salt
freshly ground black pepper
2 oz. goat cheese
¼ cup plain low-fat yogurt
2 tbsp. whole milk

Preheat the broiler. Bring 3 quarts of water to a boil in a large saucepan.

Meanwhile, mix 1 tablespoon of the oil with 1 tablespoon of the lime juice and brush the mixture over both sides of the eggplant slices. Set the slices on a baking sheet and broil them on one side until they are lightly browned — three to four minutes. Turn the slices over and broil them on the second side. Let the slices cool somewhat before transferring them to a large bowl. Put the bowl into the refrigerator.

Add the spinach rotini to the boiling water with 1½ teaspoons of salt. Start testing the pasta for doneness after 10 minutes and cook it until it is *al dente*. Drain the pasta, rinse it under cold running water, and drain it again. Add the pasta to the bowl with the eggplant.

While the pasta is cooking, cut the tomatoes into strips: Place a tomato, stem end down, on a clean work surface. With a small, sharp knife, cut the flesh from the tomato in wide, flat sections; discard the pulpy core and seeds. Slice the sections of flesh lengthwise into strips about ¼ inch wide and set them aside. Repeat the process to cut up the other tomato.

Heat the remaining tablespoon of oil in a large, heavy-bottomed skillet over medium-high heat. When the oil is hot, add the squash and shallots. Cook the vegetables, stirring frequently, for one minute. Add ▶

the shrimp, thyme, salt, some pepper and the remaining 1½ tablespoons of lime juice, and sauté the mixture until the shrimp are just cooked through — about two minutes. Stir in the tomato strips and cook the mixture for 30 seconds more. Transfer the contents of the skillet to the bowl with the pasta and eggplant, and toss the mixture well; return the bowl to the refrigerator.

To prepare the dressing, put the cheese, yogurt, milk and a liberal grinding of black pepper into a blender or food processor. Purée the mixture, scraping down the sides at least once. Add the dressing to the salad; toss the salad well and chill it briefly before serving.

Orzo with Pistachio Pesto

Serves 8 as a side dish
Working time: about 15 minutes
Total time: about 35 minutes

Calories **160**
Protein **6g.**
Cholesterol **3mg.**
Total fat **5g.**
Saturated fat **1g.**
Sodium **140mg.**

½ lb. orzo or farfalline
1 yellow pepper, seeded, deribbed and cut into small dice
2 tbsp. white wine vinegar
Pistachio pesto
1½ cups celery leaves, several leaves reserved for garnish
3 tbsp. coarsely chopped pistachio nuts (about ¾ oz.)
1 tbsp. virgin olive oil
1 garlic clove, finely chopped
½ cup unsalted chicken stock
⅓ cup freshly grated Parmesan cheese (about 1 oz.)

Add the pasta with ½ teaspoon of salt to 1 quart of boiling water. Start testing the pasta for doneness af-

ter 8 minutes and cook it until it is *al dente*.

Meanwhile, combine the yellow pepper and the vinegar in a large bowl. Drain the cooked pasta and rinse it well under cold running water. Drain the pasta again and toss it with the pepper and vinegar.

To prepare the pesto, purée the celery leaves, 2 tablespoons of the pistachios, the oil, garlic and stock in a blender or food processor, scraping down the sides from time to time. Add the Parmesan and blend the mixture just enough to incorporate the cheese.

Pour the pesto over the pasta and toss well. Garnish the salad with the reserved celery leaves and the remaining 1 tablespoon of pistachios. Serve cold.

Chinese Pasta and Long Bean Salad

Serves 8 as a side dish
Working (and total) time: about 30 minutes

Calories **150**
Protein **5g.**
Cholesterol **0mg.**
Total fat **3g.**
Saturated fat **0g.**
Sodium **20mg.**

½ lb. dried Chinese wheat noodles or dried vermicelli
½ lb. long beans or green beans, trimmed and cut into 2½-inch lengths
3 scallions, trimmed and finely chopped
1 tbsp. finely chopped cilantro
1 tbsp. roasted, unsalted peanuts, chopped
Celery-sesame dressing
½ cup chopped celery
¼ cup chopped onion
2 tbsp. rice vinegar
1 tbsp. safflower oil
1 tbsp. low-sodium soy sauce
1 tbsp. finely chopped fresh ginger
1 tsp. dark sesame oil
1 clove garlic, finely chopped
2 tbsp. fresh lemon juice
¼ tsp. chili paste

Bring 4 quarts of water to a boil in a large pot. Add the pasta and cook it until it is *al dente* — about three minutes for fresh noodles, or five minutes for dried vermicelli. Drain the pasta and rinse it under cold running water. Transfer it to a large bowl of cold water and set it aside.

Bring 2 quarts of water to a boil in a large saucepan. Add the beans and blanch them until they are just tender — about three minutes. Drain the beans and refresh them under cold running water. Drain them again and set them aside.

To make the dressing, put the celery, onion, vinegar, safflower oil, soy sauce, ginger, sesame oil, garlic, lemon juice and chili paste into a blender or food processor. Purée the dressing until it is smooth.

Drain the pasta well and transfer it to a bowl. Pour in the dressing, scallions and cilantro, and toss. Heap the dressed noodles or vermicelli in the center of a round platter or serving dish, then poke the beans one at a time into the mound to form a sunburst pattern. Sprinkle on the peanuts. Serve the salad at once.

Rotini with Spring Vegetables

Serves 8 as a first course
Working time: about 40 minutes
Total time: about 1 hour

Calories **170**
Protein **5g.**
Cholesterol **0mg.**
Total fat **4g.**
Saturated fat **1g.**
Sodium **175mg.**

1 cup unsalted veal, chicken or vegetable stock
½ lb. fresh shiitake mushrooms, wiped clean and cut into ½-inch pieces
1 large onion (about ½ lb.), halved, each half quartered
½ tsp. salt
2 tbsp. virgin olive oil
¼ cup red wine vinegar
3 carrots
2 tbsp. fresh lemon juice
½ lb. asparagus, trimmed and sliced diagonally into 1-inch lengths
½ lb. rotini or other fancy pasta
¼ cup thinly sliced fresh basil leaves
freshly ground black pepper

Heat ¾ cup of the stock in a large, nonreactive skillet over medium heat. Add the mushrooms, onion chunks and ¼ teaspoon of the salt. Bring the mixture to a simmer, reduce the heat to low, and cover the pan. Cook the vegetables for five minutes. Remove the lid and continue cooking the vegetables, stirring frequently, until all the stock has evaporated. Stir in 1 tablespoon of the olive oil and cook the mixture for three minutes more.

Transfer the contents of the skillet to a large bowl and return the skillet to the stove over low heat. Pour the vinegar and the remaining ¼ cup of stock into the skillet. Simmer the liquid, scraping the bottom of the pan with a wooden spoon to dislodge any pan deposits, until only 2 tablespoons of liquid remain. Stir the reduced liquid into the mushrooms and onions in the bowl; set the bowl aside.

Bring 2 quarts of water to a boil in a saucepan. While the water heats, prepare the carrots: Cut off the tip of each one at an oblique angle. Roll the carrot a quarter or third turn, and with the knife still at the same angle, cut again. Continue rolling and cutting until you near the end of the carrot.

Add to the boiling water 1 tablespoon of the lemon juice, ¼ teaspoon of salt and the roll-cut carrots. Boil the carrots until they are barely tender — about six minutes. Add the asparagus pieces and boil them for 30 seconds. With a slotted spoon, transfer the vegetables to a colander; do not discard the cooking liquid. Refresh the carrots and asparagus under cold running water; when they are thoroughly cooled, drain them well and toss them with the mushrooms and onions.

Refrigerate the vegetables while you finish the salad.

Return the water in the saucepan to a full boil; add the pasta and the remaining tablespoon of lemon juice. Start testing the pasta for doneness after 10 minutes and cook it until it is *al dente*. Drain the pasta and rinse it under cold running water. Drain it again.

Add the pasta to the vegetables along with the remaining tablespoon of olive oil, the basil, the remaining ¼ teaspoon of salt and a generous grinding of pepper. Toss the salad well and chill it for 10 minutes before serving.

Chilled Rice Noodle Salad

Serves 4 as a main course at lunch
Working time: about 15 minutes
Total time: about 1 hour (includes chilling)

Calories **375**
Protein **14g.**
Cholesterol **25mg.**
Total fat **10g.**
Saturated fat **3g.**
Sodium **210mg.**

6 oz. boneless pork loin, julienned
¼ cup rice vinegar
1 tbsp. finely chopped garlic
1 tbsp. finely chopped fresh ginger
2 tsp. Chinese five-spice powder
¼ cup cream sherry
½ lb. sugar snap peas or snow peas, stems and strings removed
1 tbsp. safflower oil
½ lb. dried rice noodles
¼ tsp. salt
freshly ground black pepper
½ tsp. dark sesame oil

Put the pork in a small heatproof bowl and set it aside. Combine the vinegar, garlic, ginger, five-spice powder and sherry in a small saucepan, and bring the mixture to a simmer. Pour the marinade over the pork and let it cool to room temperature — about 15 minutes.

Meanwhile, if you are using sugar-snap peas, blanch them in boiling water until they are just tender — about four minutes; if you are using snow peas, blanch them for only 30 seconds. Refresh the peas under cold running water, then drain them well and transfer them to a large bowl.

Drain the pork, reserving the marinade for the dressing. Heat the safflower oil in a heavy-bottomed skillet over medium-high heat. Add the pork and sauté it until it loses its pink hue — three to four minutes. With a slotted spoon, transfer the pork to the bowl containing the peas. Pour the reserved marinade into the skillet and bring it to a boil; cook the marinade for one minute. Remove the skillet from the heat and set it aside. ▶

Add the noodles to 3 quarts of boiling water with 1 teaspoon of salt. Start testing the noodles for doneness after four minutes and cook them until they are *al dente*. Drain the noodles and rinse them under cold running water; drain them again and add them to the pork and peas. Pour the reserved marinade over the noodle mixture, then add the ¼ teaspoon of salt, some pepper and the sesame oil. Toss the salad well and refrigerate it for at least 20 minutes before serving it.

EDITOR'S NOTE: *A variation of Chinese five-spice powder may be made at home by chopping in a blender equal parts of Sichuan peppercorns, fennel seeds, ground cloves and ground cinnamon.*

Wagon-Wheel Pasta Salad

Serves 12 as a first course
Working (and total) time: about 35 minutes

Calories **210**
Protein **7g.**
Cholesterol **0mg.**
Total fat **4g.**
Saturated fat **1g.**
Sodium **170mg.**

8 sun-dried tomatoes
1 lb. wagon wheels (or other fancy pasta)
2 cups fresh lima beans, or 10 oz. frozen baby lima beans
2 garlic cloves, peeled
¼ cup red wine vinegar
¼ tsp. salt
freshly ground black pepper
2 tbsp. cut chives
4 cherry tomatoes, cut into quarters
1 tbsp. virgin olive oil

Put the sun-dried tomatoes into a small heatproof bowl and pour ½ cup of boiling water over them. Let the tomatoes soak for 20 minutes.

While the tomatoes are soaking, cook the pasta and lima beans: Add the pasta to 4 quarts of boiling water with 1 teaspoon of salt. Begin testing the pasta for doneness after five minutes and cook it until it is *al dente*. Drain the pasta and rinse it under cold running water; drain it once more and transfer the pasta to a large bowl. Add the fresh lima beans to 1 quart of boiling water and cook them until they are barely tender — eight to 10 minutes. Drain the beans and set them aside. (If you are using frozen limas, cook them in ¼ cup of boiling water for five minutes.)

In a blender or food processor, purée the sun-dried tomatoes along with their soaking liquid, the garlic, vinegar, salt and some pepper. Add the lima beans, chives, cherry tomatoes, oil and tomato-garlic purée to the pasta; toss well and serve the salad immediately.

Pasta Salad with Black Bean Sauce

Serves 8 as a main course at lunch
Working time: about 15 minutes
Total time: about 1 hour and 30 minutes
(includes chilling)

Calories **290**
Protein **12g.**
Cholesterol **0mg.**
Total fat **7g.**
Saturated fat **1g.**
Sodium **495mg.**

1 lb. vermicelli (or other thin pasta)
2 tbsp. peanut oil
2 small dried hot red chili peppers, coarsely chopped (caution, page 17)
3 scallions, trimmed and sliced diagonally
2 garlic cloves, finely chopped
½ cup fermented black beans, rinsed (about 1 oz.)
½ lb. firm tofu, cut into ¾-inch cubes
½ cup unsalted chicken stock
2 celery stalks, sliced diagonally
¼ tsp. salt
4 tsp. rice vinegar

Add the vermicelli with 1 teaspoon of salt to 4 quarts of boiling water. Start testing the pasta after five minutes and cook it until it is *al dente*. Drain the pasta, transfer

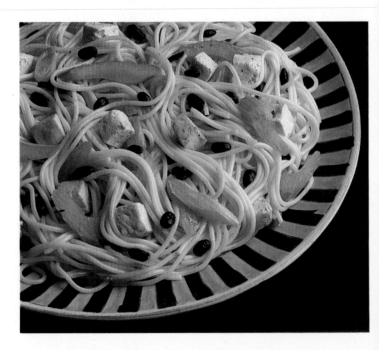

it to a large bowl of cold water, and set it aside while you make the sauce.

To begin the sauce, heat the peanut oil and chili peppers in a small saucepan; when the oil begins to smoke, remove the pan from the heat and set it aside to cool for about five minutes. Strain the oil into a heavy-bottomed skillet. Discard the chili peppers.

Put the scallions and garlic into the skillet containing the peanut oil; cook them over medium heat for two minutes. Add the black beans, tofu and stock, and simmer the mixture for five minutes. Stir in the celery and salt, and continue cooking the mixture until the celery is barely tender — about two minutes more.

While the sauce is simmering, drain the noodles well. Transfer the noodles to a large bowl and toss them with the vinegar. Pour the hot sauce over all and mix thoroughly. Refrigerate the salad for at least one hour before serving.

Buckwheat Noodle Salad

Serves 8 as a first course
Working (and total) time: about 25 minutes

Calories **130**
Protein **3g.**
Cholesterol **0mg.**
Total fat **3g.**
Saturated fat **0g.**
Sodium **135mg.**

½ lb. dried buckwheat noodles (soba)
1 sweet red pepper, seeded, deribbed and julienned
3 Nappa cabbage leaves, torn into small pieces
Ginger-lime dressing
1-inch piece of fresh ginger, peeled and coarsely chopped
1 lime, the zest grated and the juice reserved
¼ tsp. salt
½ tsp. honey
1 small shallot, finely chopped
1½ tbsp. safflower oil
½ tsp. dark sesame oil

Add the noodles to 8 cups of boiling water in a large saucepan. Start testing them for doneness after five minutes and cook them until they are *al dente*. Drain the noodles and rinse them well; then cover them with cold water and set them aside.

To make the dressing, place the ginger, lime zest and salt in a mortar; mash them with a pestle until the ginger is reduced to very small pieces. Stir in the lime juice, honey, shallot, safflower oil and sesame oil.

Drain the noodles thoroughly and transfer them to a serving platter. Pour the dressing over the noodles and toss them with the pepper strips. Serve the salad immediately, surrounded by the cabbage.

Ditalini Salad with Smoked Salmon

Serves 8 as a first course or side dish
Working time: about 20 minutes
Total time: about 30 minutes

Calories **130**
Protein **5g.**
Cholesterol **3mg.**
Total fat **1g.**
Saturated fat **0g.**
Sodium **110mg.**

½ lb. ditalini or elbow macaroni
½ cup plain low-fat yogurt
1 tbsp. brown sugar
¾ tsp. dry mustard
2 tbsp. cut fresh dill
2 tbsp. fresh lemon juice
¼ tsp. salt
freshly ground black pepper
1 oz. smoked salmon, cut into ¼-inch cubes

Add the pasta to 4 quarts of boiling water with 1½ teaspoons of salt. Begin testing the pasta after five minutes and cook it until it is *al dente*. Drain the pasta and rinse it under cold running water; drain it once more and transfer it to a large bowl.

To prepare the dressing, whisk together the yogurt, brown sugar, mustard, dill, lemon juice, salt and some pepper in a small bowl.

Add the salmon to the pasta, pour the dressing over all, and toss well; serve the salad immediately.

EDITOR'S NOTE: *Both the dressing and pasta may be prepared an hour before serving time; they should be refrigerated separately and assembled at the last possible moment.*

Pasta Salad with Tomato-Anchovy Sauce

Serves 6 as a side dish
Working time: about 1 hour and 15 minutes
Total time: about 2 hours and 15 minutes

Calories **135**
Protein **4g.**
Cholesterol **0mg.**
Total fat **3g.**
Saturated fat **0g.**
Sodium **45mg.**

1 tbsp. virgin olive oil
¼ cup finely chopped red onion
1 garlic clove, finely chopped
½ tsp. paprika, preferably Hungarian
¼ tsp. cinnamon
¼ tsp. ground cumin
cayenne pepper
freshly ground black pepper
4 ripe tomatoes (about 1½ lb.), peeled, seeded and chopped
2 anchovies, rinsed, patted dry with paper towels and cut into pieces
1 tsp. red wine vinegar
4 small carrots (about ¼ lb.), peeled and cut into bâtonnets
¼ lb. green beans, trimmed and cut into 1½-inch lengths
2 yellow or sweet red peppers
¼ lb. penne or ziti
2 tbsp. chopped fresh basil

To prepare the tomato sauce, heat the oil in a large, heavy-bottomed skillet over medium heat. Add the onion and garlic and sauté them, stirring frequently, until the onion is translucent — about five minutes. Add the paprika, cinnamon, cumin, a pinch of cayenne pepper and some black pepper; continue sautéing, stirring constantly, for 30 seconds. Stir in the tomatoes and anchovy pieces, and raise the heat to medium high. Bring the sauce to a simmer and cook it, stirring frequently, until it is thickened — about 12 minutes. Remove the skillet from the heat and stir in the vinegar. Set the sauce aside and let it cool thoroughly.

While the sauce is thickening, cook the vegetables: Pour enough water into a saucepan to fill it about 1 inch deep. Set a vegetable steamer in the pan and bring the water to a boil. Put the carrots and green beans into the steamer, cover the pan, and steam the vegetables until they are tender — two to three minutes. Refresh the vegetables under cold running water; drain them and set them aside.

Roast the yellow or red peppers about 2 inches below a preheated broiler, turning them until they are blistered on all sides. Place the peppers in a bowl and cover the bowl with plastic wrap; the trapped steam will loosen their skins. Peel and seed the peppers, then cut them into ½-inch squares.

Add the pasta to 2 quarts of boiling water with ½ teaspoon of salt. Start testing the pasta after eight minutes and cook it until it is *al dente*. Drain the pasta and rinse it under cold running water, then drain it again. Transfer the pasta to a large bowl. Add the tomato sauce along with the carrots, beans, pepper pieces and basil; toss the salad well. Let the salad stand at room temperature for one hour before serving it.

3

The basic materials of meat and seafood salads set the stage for fresh herbs to play their roles as complements and counterpoints.

The Ingredients of Success

Any book as full of vegetable-based recipes as this one should, for the sake of balance, include salads made with meat, poultry, fish and shellfish. Not only is there pure eating pleasure to recommend them; there is also the nutrition they provide. Saltwater fish and shellfish contribute iodine, phosphorus and other valuable minerals to the diet; both meat and poultry rank high in the various B vitamins and iron.

Almost any recipe in this section is worthy of star billing on the table. If many take longer to prepare than some in the preceding sections, they repay the extra time spent on them, for most can be served as main courses. Beautifully garnished or artfully arranged, they will satisfy the eye, please the appetite, and delight guests or family. Moreover, they make for cool summer eating when hot food can seem too much of a good thing.

If you plan to serve the salads as main courses, you may wish to supplement them with bread, rolls or other starchy foods, and you may want to include another salad, perhaps one made of leafy greens or of vegetables for additional fiber, vitamins and minerals.

The dishes are calculated to be healthful. Pork and lamb, two meats generally not associated with salads, are used, as well as beef. The cuts are lean, and any visible fat is removed; cooking the meat slowly by such methods as roasting, braising and poaching guarantees that fat will be rendered from the tissue; the fat can then be skimmed from the cooking liquid. Poultry is skinned to remove fat and cooked gently to preserve succulence and flavor.

The recipes are also innovative. In a departure from tradition, a fish terrine — usually presented in solitary splendor as a first course — serves as the focus of an elegant salad. In another break, vegetables are roasted with shellfish in a little oil and served tender but still crisp. Meat is sometimes added to the salads in slices, rather than in pieces. To enhance the flavor of the salads themselves, the cooking juices are often blended into the dressings. And when it comes to some old salad stand-bys, such as turkey, chicken and crab, the inclusion of ingredients as different as peaches, barley and jícama elevates them to new status.

Scandinavian-Style
Bluefish Salad

Serves 6 as a main course
Working time: about 40 minutes
Total time: about 3 hours and 15 minutes
(includes marinating)

Calories **535**
Protein **36g.**
Cholesterol **90mg.**
Total fat **14g.**
Saturated fat **4g.**
Sodium **430mg.**

1 cup sugar
2 cups white wine vinegar
2 small red onions, thinly sliced
freshly ground black pepper
½ tsp. mustard seeds
2 bay leaves
one 3½-lb. bluefish, dressed and cut into 1-inch-thick steaks
4 boiling potatoes (about 1½ lbs.), peeled and sliced
3 carrots, sliced into thin rounds
2 tbsp. chopped fresh dill, or 2 tsp. dried dill
1 cucumber, preferably unwaxed
6 radishes, thinly sliced
1 head of Boston lettuce, or 2 heads of Bibb lettuce, washed and dried
Pumpernickel toast
2 tbsp. unsalted butter
2 tbsp. grated red onion
½ tsp. caraway seeds
12 slices dark pumpernickel bread

Put the sugar, vinegar, half of the onions, some pepper, the mustard seeds and the bay leaves into a small, nonreactive saucepan. Bring the liquid to a boil, reduce the heat, and simmer the marinade for 10 minutes.

Set the bluefish steaks in a nonreactive heatproof dish large enough to hold them in a single layer. Strain the marinade over them, discarding the solids. Simmer the fish over medium heat for two minutes. Remove the dish from the heat and allow it to cool to room temperature — about 30 minutes.

Pour enough water into a saucepan to fill it about 1 inch deep. Set a vegetable steamer in the pan and bring the water to a boil. Put the potatoes into the steamer, cover the pan tightly, and steam the potatoes until they are tender — about six minutes. Add the potatoes to the fish. Steam the carrots in the same way, but for only three minutes. Add the carrots to the fish and potatoes. Sprinkle the dill over the fish and vegetables, cover the dish, and refrigerate the mixture for at least two hours.

Shortly before serving the salad, score the cucumber lengthwise with a channel knife or a paring knife. Slice the cucumber into thin rounds and add them to the fish along with the radishes and the remaining onion.

To make the toast, first preheat the oven to 450° F. Mix together the butter, grated onion, caraway seeds and some pepper. Spread this mixture on the pumpernickel slices, then toast them in the oven for about four minutes.

Using a slotted spoon, transfer the salad to a serving dish lined with the lettuce leaves. Pour about half the marinade over the salad; discard the remainder. Serve the salad accompanied by the pumpernickel toast.

Seviche Salad

THIS RECIPE CALLS FOR ¼ CUP OF SUGAR; IT IS ADDED TO THE WATER USED FOR BLANCHING ORANGE ZEST, THEN DISCARDED.

Serves 8 as a main course
Working time: about 45 minutes
Total time: about one day (includes marinating time)

Calories **210**
Protein **22g.**
Cholesterol **47mg.**
Total fat **7g.**
Saturated fat **1g.**
Sodium **380mg.**

4 oranges
¼ cup sugar
3 limes
3 lemons
3 celery stalks, thinly sliced
1 green pepper, seeded, deribbed and julienned
1 yellow pepper, seeded, deribbed and julienned
1 small red onion, thinly sliced
1 garlic clove, finely chopped
2 tbsp. chopped cilantro
1 tsp. salt
½ tsp. black pepper
hot red-pepper sauce
½ tsp. ground cumin
¼ tsp. cumin seeds
1 lb. bay scallops, the bright, white connective tissue removed, the scallops rinsed and patted dry
1 lb. halibut fillets, rinsed, patted dry and cut into ½ inch cubes
¼ lb. spinach, washed, stemmed and dried, or 1 head of oakleaf lettuce, washed and dried
2 tbsp. chopped parsley, preferably Italian
2 tbsp. virgin olive oil

Using a vegetable peeler, remove the zest from one orange, leaving behind as much of the pith as possible. Cut the zest into fine julienne, then put it into a small saucepan with 1½ cups of water and the sugar. Bring the water to a boil and cook the zest for 2 minutes. Drain the zest and transfer it to a large, nonreactive bowl. Into another bowl, squeeze the juice from the oranges, limes and lemons, strain it and set it aside.

Add the celery, green and yellow peppers, onion, garlic, cilantro, salt, pepper, a few drops of red-pepper sauce, the ground cumin and cumin seeds to the bowl. Gently toss the contents of the bowl with the scallops and the halibut cubes. Pour the citrus juices over all and toss again. Press down on the solid ingredients so that they are completely submerged. Cover the bowl and let the seviche marinate in the refrigerator for 8 hours.

Use a slotted spoon to transfer the seviche to a platter or individual plates lined with the spinach or lettuce. Pour ½ cup of the marinade into a small bowl. Add the parsley; then, whisking constantly, pour in the oil in a slow, steady stream. Spoon the dressing over the salad and serve immediately.

Toss the leek, carrot and celery in a bowl with a generous grinding of black pepper; set the bowl aside.

To prepare the dressing, combine the mustard, the dill, some pepper and the tablespoon of lemon juice in a small bowl. Whisking vigorously, pour in the oil in a thin, steady stream; continue whisking until the dressing is thoroughly combined, then set the bowl aside.

Add the linguine with ½ teaspoon of salt to 4 quarts of boiling water. Start testing the pasta for doneness after eight minutes and cook it until it is *al dente*. Drain the pasta and rinse it under cold running water, then transfer it to a large bowl and toss it with half of the dressing; set the bowl aside.

Pour enough water into a wok or large skillet to fill it about 1 inch deep. Put the julienned vegetables in a bamboo steamer and set the steamer in the wok or skillet. (If you lack a bamboo steamer, steam the vegetables on a plate set on a wire rack in the bottom of a large skillet.) Bring the water to a boil, tightly cover the wok or skillet, and steam the vegetables for about one minute. Place the fish pieces on top of the vegetables, cover the pan again and steam the fish until it is opaque and feels firm to the touch — one to two minutes. Remove the steamer or plate and let the fish and vegetables cool.

To present the salad, first mound the linguine on a serving platter. Top the pasta with the cooled fish and vegetables. Pour the remaining dressing over the salad and serve immediately.

Orange Roughy Salad with Green and White Linguine

Serves 4 as a main course
Working time: about 50 minutes
Total time: about 1 hour and 15 minutes

Calories **440**
Protein **30g.**
Cholesterol **45mg.**
Total fat **10g.**
Saturated fat **1g.**
Sodium **290mg.**

1 lb. orange roughy or monkfish fillets, rinsed, patted dry and cut into 1 by 2 inch pieces
juice of 1 lemon
1 tbsp. chopped fresh thyme, or 1 tsp. dried thyme leaves
⅛ tsp. cayenne pepper
¼ tsp. salt
freshly ground black pepper
2 leeks, trimmed, split, washed thoroughly to remove all grit, and julienned
1 carrot, julienned
1 celery stalk, julienned
¼ lb. spinach linguine
¼ lb. linguine
Dill dressing
½ tsp. Dijon mustard
1 tbsp. finely cut fresh dill, or 2 tsp. dried dill
freshly ground black pepper
1 tbsp. fresh lemon juice
2 tbsp. safflower oil

Place the fish pieces in a shallow dish. In a small bowl, combine the juice of the lemon with the thyme, cayenne pepper, salt and some black pepper. Pour the lemon marinade over the fish and let the fish marinate for at least 30 minutes.

Chilled Fish Salad with Okra

Serves 4 as a main course
Working time: about 45 minutes
Total time: about 1 hour and 45 minutes

Calories **350**
Protein **26g.**
Cholesterol **48mg.**
Total fat **9g.**
Saturated fat **1g.**
Sodium **235mg.**

1 bunch scallions, trimmed, the green parts left whole, the white parts thinly sliced
3 bay leaves
1 cup red wine vinegar
1 lb. thin cod fillets (or black sea bass), rinsed and cut crosswise into pieces about 3 inches long
2 tbsp. tomato paste
3 large ripe tomatoes (about 1 ½ lb.), peeled, seeded and coarsely chopped
2 tsp. sugar
¼ tsp. salt
3 tbsp. chopped fresh parsley
2 tbsp. chopped fresh oregano, or 2 tsp. dried oregano
1 lb. fresh peas, shelled, or 1 cup frozen peas, defrosted
1 cup fresh corn (from about 1 large ear), or 1 cup frozen corn, defrosted
1 ½ cups okra (about 6 oz.), trimmed and cut into ½-inch rounds
2 tbsp. safflower oil
1 cup cornmeal
1 tbsp. cayenne pepper

Pour 6 cups of water into a large, nonreactive saucepan set over medium heat. Add the scallion greens, bay leaves and ½ cup of the vinegar, and simmer the liquid for 15 minutes.

Arrange the fish pieces in a single layer in a shallow dish. Strain the hot liquid over the fish; let the dish stand at room temperature for 20 minutes before refrigerating it for half an hour.

Meanwhile, whisk together the tomato paste and the remaining ½ cup of vinegar. Stir in the white scallion parts, then the tomatoes, sugar, salt, parsley and oregano. Chill the relish for 30 minutes.

Pour enough water into a saucepan to fill it about 1 inch deep. Set a vegetable steamer in the pan and bring the water to a boil. Add the fresh peas to the steamer, cover the pan and cook the peas until they are just tender — three to four minutes. Add the fresh corn to the peas and steam the vegetables for one minute more. (Frozen peas and corn do not require steaming.) Transfer the peas and corn to a bowl, and set the bowl in the refrigerator for half an hour.

Add the okra to the steamer and cook it for 30 seconds. Set the okra aside at room temperature until just before serving time.

Drain the liquid from the chilled fish. Carefully arrange a layer each of the relish, the peas and corn, and the fish in a large bowl. Top the fish with another layer of relish, then with a final layer of peas and corn.

Heat the oil in a large, heavy-bottomed skillet over medium-high heat. Combine the cornmeal with the cayenne pepper and toss the okra in this mixture; shake off the excess. Add the okra to the skillet and fry it, stirring constantly, until it is brown on all sides. Scatter the okra over the salad and serve immediately.

Monkfish, Lima Bean and Red Cabbage Salad

Serves 4 as a main course
Working time: about 20 minutes
Total time: about 1 hour (includes chilling)

Calories **240**
Protein **25g.**
Cholesterol **40mg.**
Total fat **6g.**
Saturated fat **0g.**
Sodium **365mg.**

1 lb. monkfish fillet, trimmed, rinsed and patted dry
¼ tsp. salt
⅛ tsp. white pepper
2 cups fresh lima beans, or 10 oz. frozen baby lima beans, thawed
1 cup thinly sliced red cabbage
2 tbsp. chopped fresh mint, or 2 tsp. dried mint
3 tbsp. fish stock or unsalted chicken stock
2 tbsp. sherry vinegar
1 tbsp. safflower oil
1 tbsp. chopped parsley
1 head of leaf lettuce, washed and dried

Cut the monkfish fillet crosswise into thin slices. Season the slices with the salt and some pepper.

Pour enough water into a saucepan to fill it about 1 inch deep. Set a vegetable steamer in the pan and bring the water to a boil. Put the monkfish slices into the steamer, tightly cover the pan, and steam the fish until it is opaque and firm to the touch — two to three minutes. Transfer the monkfish slices to a large, shallow dish.

If you are using fresh lima beans, cook them in 1 quart of boiling water until they are barely tender — eight to 10 minutes — then drain them and add them to the monkfish. (Frozen beans require no cooking.) Blanch the cabbage in 4 cups of boiling water for three minutes; drain the cabbage and add it to the monkfish and beans.

To prepare the dressing, whisk together the mint, stock, vinegar and oil. Pour the dressing over the contents of the dish; mix the ingredients thoroughly, then refrigerate the salad for 30 minutes.

Add the parsley to the salad and toss. Serve the salad on a bed of lettuce.

Fish and Vegetable Terrine

Serves 12 as a first course
Working time: about 1 hour and 15 minutes
Total time: about 8 hours (includes chilling)

Calories **125**
Protein **10g.**
Cholesterol **28mg.**
Total fat **7g.**
Saturated fat **1g.**
Sodium **190mg.**

2 shallots, chopped
½ cup fish stock or unsalted chicken stock
12 saffron threads
1 lb. flounder fillets, rinsed, patted dry and cut into 1-inch chunks
¼ lb. smoked salmon, coarsely chopped
2 egg whites
5 tsp. chopped fresh tarragon, or 2½ tsp. dried tarragon
cayenne pepper
½ cup half-and-half
16 green beans, trimmed
4 carrots, peeled and quartered lengthwise
12 large leaves of romaine lettuce, washed and dried
6 oz. radicchio, washed and dried, or 2 bunches of watercress, stemmed, washed and dried
6 tbsp. vinaigrette (recipe, page 13)
1 tbsp. fresh lemon juice

Put the shallots, stock and saffron into a small saucepan. Bring the mixture to a simmer and cook it for 10 minutes. Set the mixture aside and let it cool to room temperature.

Purée the flounder and smoked salmon in a food processor. Add the shallot mixture and purée again. With the motor running, add the egg whites, 2 teaspoons of the fresh tarragon or 1 teaspoon of the dried tarragon, and a pinch of cayenne pepper. Press the mixture through a medium sieve into a bowl. Set the bowl in a pan of ice. With a wooden spoon, incorporate the half-and-half into the fish mixture 2 tablespoons at a time. Refrigerate the mixture, covered, while you prepare the remaining ingredients.

Preheat the oven to 325° F.

Pour enough water into a saucepan to fill it about 1 inch deep. Set a vegetable steamer in the pan and bring the water to a boil. Put the beans into the steamer, cover the pan tightly, and steam the beans until they are tender — about three minutes. Remove the beans from the steamer, refresh them under cold running water, drain them, and set them aside. Then steam the carrots the same way until they are tender — about six minutes. Refresh and drain the carrots, and set them aside.

Bring a large pot of water to a boil. Blanch the lettuce leaves in the boiling water until they are limp — about one minute. Remove the leaves with a slotted spoon and drain them on paper towels. When the leaves are cool enough to handle, use a paring knife to trim away the thickest part of each leaf's center rib.

Lightly oil a 5-cup ceramic or glass loaf pan. Line the pan with the romaine leaves, overlapping them slightly. Allow the tips of the leaves to overhang the sides; the tips will later be folded over to enclose the terrine. ▶

Spread one quarter of the fish purée in the bottom of the loaf pan. Arrange half of the carrot quarters on top of the fish purée and parallel to the pan's sides, leaving a ½-inch border uncovered around the edge.

Spread one third of the remaining purée over the carrots, covering them entirely. Arrange the beans in a single layer in the terrine as you did the first layer of carrots. Spread half of the remaining fish over the beans; arrange another layer of carrots atop the purée and top off the assembly with the remaining fish. Fold over the lettuce leaves to encase the terrine snugly. Rap the loaf pan sharply on the work surface to eliminate any trapped air pockets.

Cover the pan with aluminum foil. Using a skewer, poke two holes in the foil; set the terrine in a roasting pan filled halfway with boiling water. Transfer the pan to the oven and bake the terrine for one hour. Remove the roasting pan from the oven and let the terrine rest, still in the roasting pan, for one hour. Remove the loaf pan from the roasting pan and refrigerate the terrine for five hours before serving it.

To unmold the terrine, cover the loaf pan with a small cutting board and turn both over together; gently lift away the pan. Slice the terrine into 12 serving pieces. Arrange the radicchio or watercress on 12 individual plates; set a slice of terrine on each plate. Whisk together the vinaigrette, the remaining tarragon and the lemon juice. Drizzle a little of the dressing over each portion and serve at once.

Fish Rolled in Nori

Serves 6 as a first course
Working time: about 25 minutes
Total time: about 40 minutes

Calories **115**
Protein **14g.**
Cholesterol **28mg.**
Total fat **4g.**
Saturated fat **1g.**
Sodium **105mg.**

4 scallions, trimmed
¾ lb. sole fillets, rinsed, patted dry and cut into 1-inch chunks
1 garlic clove, chopped
1 tsp. finely chopped fresh ginger
1 egg white
6 drops hot red-pepper sauce
⅛ tsp. white pepper
⅓ cup fish stock or unsalted chicken stock
3 sheets nori
1 large carrot, cut into 2-inch segments, each segment halved lengthwise and cut into ¼-inch-thick strips
4 oz. mâche, washed and dried, or 4 oz. spinach, washed, stemmed and dried
2 tbsp. mirin (sweetened Japanese rice wine)
1 tbsp. rice vinegar
¼ tsp. dark sesame oil
1 tbsp. peanut oil

Cut the green tops off the scallions and julienne enough of them to yield about 1 tablespoon. Set the julienne aside. Coarsely chop the white parts of the scallions and transfer them to a food processor or a blender. Add the fish chunks, garlic, ginger, egg white, red-pepper sauce, white pepper and stock; purée the mixture, pausing occasionally to scrape down the sides, until no large pieces of fish remain.

Place a sheet of nori, its shiny side down, on a work surface. Spread ⅓ cup of the fish mixture along one of the shorter edges of the sheet, forming a ribbon about 1 inch wide. Lay a line of carrot strips end to end down the center of the ribbon. Press down lightly on the carrot strips to anchor them in the mixture. Starting at the edge with the purée on it, roll up the nori to enclose the fish mixture. Cut off the excess nori — about half a sheet — and use it to make another fish roll. Use the remaining nori sheets, fish mixture and carrot strips to fashion a total of six rolls.

Pour enough water into a deep skillet to fill it to a depth of about 2 inches. Bring the water to a boil, then reduce the heat to maintain a gentle simmer. Lower the nori rolls into the water and poach them until the fish is cooked — four to five minutes. To test for doneness, gently remove one of the rolls from the water with a slotted spoon and cut a slice from each end; the fish purée should be opaque. Remove the rolls from the water and allow them to cool to room temperature, then slice them into rounds about ½ inch thick. Arrange a line of rounds on each individual salad plate and place the mâche or spinach on either side.

Whisk together the mirin, rice vinegar, sesame oil, and peanut oil; pour some of this dressing over each portion. Garnish with the scallion julienne and serve the salads at once.

Trout Salad with Basil Vinaigrette

Serves 4 as a first course
Working time: about 20 minutes
Total time: about 40 minutes

Calories **200**	two 1-lb. trout, filleted
Protein **22g.**	2 tbsp. sherry vinegar
Cholesterol **64mg.**	1 tbsp. finely chopped shallot
Total fat **10g.**	1 small garlic clove, finely chopped
Saturated fat **1g.**	¼ tsp. salt
Sodium **185mg.**	⅛ tsp. white pepper
	1 tbsp. safflower oil
	¼ cup loosely packed fresh basil leaves, cut into chiffonade (technique, page 51)
	2 ripe plum tomatoes, each cut lengthwise into six slices
	4 sprigs fresh basil

Lay a trout fillet on a cutting board with its skinned side down. With a small knife, cut along one side of the line of bones running the length of the fillet. Make a similar cut along the other side of the line of bones; discard the thin strip of flesh and bones thus formed. You should now have two pieces, one twice the width of the other. Halve the larger piece lengthwise. Fold each piece into a loose "bow" and set the bow on a heat-proof plate. Repeat these steps to fashion the remaining fillets into bows.

Pour enough water into a large pot to fill it about 1 inch deep. Place two or three small bowls of equal height in the bottom of the pot; set the plate on top of the bowls. Cover the pot, bring the water to a boil, and steam the fish until it is opaque and firm to the touch — about two minutes. Remove the plate and set it aside while you prepare the dressing.

Whisk together the vinegar, shallot, garlic, salt, pepper, oil and half of the basil. Pour this dressing over the fish bows and refrigerate them until they are cool — about 20 minutes.

Arrange three tomato slices on each of four plates. Use a spatula to transfer a bow onto each tomato slice. Sprinkle the salads with the remaining chiffonade of basil. Drizzle the chilled dressing over all, garnish with the basil sprigs, and serve at once.

Lobster Salad
with Sweet Peppers
and Cilantro

Serves 4 as a main course or 8 as a first course
Working time: about 30 minutes
Total time: about 2 hours and 30 minutes
(includes chilling and marinating)

Calories **190**
Protein **18g.**
Cholesterol **66mg.**
Total fat **8g.**
Saturated fat **1g.**
Sodium **250mg.**

2 carrots, sliced into thin rounds
1 onion, thinly sliced
⅓ cup coarsely chopped parsley, stems included
2 bay leaves
8 black peppercorns
1 tbsp. vinegar, wine or lemon juice
3 live lobsters (about 1¼ lb. each)
2 tbsp. fresh lemon juice
2 tbsp. fresh lime juice
2 tbsp. virgin olive oil
1 sweet red pepper, seeded, deribbed and cut into ¼-inch dice
1 yellow pepper, seeded, deribbed and cut into ¼-inch dice
½ hydroponic cucumber, seeded and cut into bâtonnets, or 1 regular cucumber, peeled, seeded and cut into bâtonnets
½ small red onion, chopped
1½ tbsp. chopped fresh cilantro
freshly ground black pepper
4 or 8 large red-leaf lettuce leaves, washed and dried
8 or 16 thin lemon wedges

Pour enough water into a large pot to fill it about 1 inch deep. Add the carrots, onion, parsley, bay leaves, peppercorns and vinegar, wine or lemon juice. Bring the liquid to a boil, then reduce the heat and simmer the mixture for 20 minutes. Return the liquid to a boil, add the lobsters, and cover the pot; cook the lobsters until

they turn a bright red-orange — about 15 minutes. Remove the lobsters and let them cool. When the lobsters are cool enough to handle, remove the claw and tail meat and cut the tail meat into ¾-inch slices.

Combine the lemon and lime juices in a large bowl, then whisk in the oil. Add the lobster meat, peppers, cucumber, red onion, cilantro and some pepper. Toss the mixture well, then cover the bowl. Refrigerate the salad for at least two hours to meld the flavors, stirring several times to distribute the dressing.

To serve, place a lettuce leaf on each plate; divide the lobster salad among the plates, then garnish each salad with two lemon wedges.

EDITOR'S NOTE: *If you like, the lobster-cooking liquid may be strained and reserved for another use — as a medium for boiling pasta, or as the base for a seafood stew. To give the liquid even more flavor, simmer the lobster shells in it for 20 minutes before straining it.*

Thai Lemon-Lime Shrimp Salad

Serves 4 as a main course at lunch
Working (and total) time: about 45 minutes

Calories **125**
Protein **18g.**
Cholesterol **131mg.**
Total fat **1g.**
Saturated fat **0g.**
Sodium **230mg.**

1 tart green apple, preferably Granny Smith, peeled, cored and julienned
3 tbsp. fresh lemon juice
3 tbsp. fresh lime juice
2 shallots, thinly sliced
1½ tbsp. chopped cilantro
1 tbsp. chopped fresh mint, or 1 tsp. dried mint
2 tsp. fish sauce or low-sodium soy sauce
2 garlic cloves, finely chopped
1 small dried red chili pepper, soaked in hot water for 20 minutes, drained, seeded and chopped (caution, page 17)
2 scallions, thinly sliced
1 lb. medium shrimp, peeled, deveined if necessary and halved lengthwise
2 heads of Boston lettuce, or 4 heads of Bibb lettuce, washed and dried
4 mint sprigs

Put the julienned apple into a large bowl and toss the pieces with the lemon and lime juices, shallots, cilantro, mint, fish sauce or soy sauce, garlic, chili pepper and scallions.

Bring 2 quarts of water to a boil in a saucepan. Add the shrimp and cook them until they are opaque — 30 seconds to one minute. Drain the shrimp and transfer them to the bowl. Gently mix them into the salad. Cover the bowl and refrigerate the salad for at least 30 minutes.

Serve the salad on lettuce leaves on individual plates, each portion garnished with a sprig of mint.

Shrimp and Artichoke Salad

Serves 6 as a main course at lunch
Working (and total) time: about 1 hour and 15 minutes

Calories **140**
Protein **13g.**
Cholesterol **87mg.**
Total fat **5g.**
Saturated fat **1g.**
Sodium **70mg.**

4 artichokes
1 lemon, cut in half
1 lb. medium shrimp, peeled, and deveined if necessary
¼ lb. green beans, trimmed and cut into ½-inch lengths
4 large ripe tomatoes (about 2 lb.), peeled, seeded and cut into ½-inch chunks
2 tbsp. finely cut chives
6 basil leaves, thinly sliced
1 garlic clove, finely chopped
4 tbsp. sherry vinegar or red wine vinegar
1 tsp. grainy mustard
3 tbsp. grated onion
2 tbsp. virgin olive oil

Cut the stems off the artichokes. Rub the cut surfaces with one of the lemon halves to prevent discoloration.

Bring 4 quarts of water to a boil in a large, nonreactive saucepan. Squeeze the juice of the lemon half into the water, then add the half itself. Put the artichokes into the water; reduce the heat to maintain a strong simmer, and cook the artichokes until they are tender about 20 minutes. Remove the artichokes from the water with a slotted spoon and set them aside.

Bring 2 quarts of water to a boil in a nonreactive saucepan. Add the juice from the second lemon half, and drop in the rind as well. Add the shrimp and cook them until they are opaque — 30 seconds to one minute. Drain the shrimp, refresh them under cold running water, and drain them again. Reserve six of the shrimp for garnish; cut the remainder into ¾-inch pieces. Put the shrimp pieces in a large bowl.

When the artichokes are cool enough to handle, pull off their leaves. Discard the dark green outer leaves but save the inner ones for garnish. With a teaspoon, scoop the furry choke from each bottom and discard it. Cut the bottoms into ½-inch-long pieces and add them to the shrimp.

Blanch the beans in 1 quart of boiling water until they turn bright green and are tender yet still somewhat crisp — one to two minutes. Drain the beans, refresh them under cold running water, and drain them again. Transfer the beans to the bowl containing the shrimp; add the tomatoes, chives, basil and garlic.

In a small bowl, whisk together the vinegar, mustard, onion and oil. Pour this dressing over the shrimp and beans, and toss well. Spoon the salad onto individual plates, garnishing each serving with the remaining artichoke leaves and one of the reserved whole shrimp.

Shrimp Salad on Fresh Pineapple-Mango Relish

Serves 8 as a main course at lunch
Working time: about 30 minutes
Total time: about 1 hour

Calories **160**
Protein **13g.**
Cholesterol **104mg.**
Total fat **4g.**
Saturated fat **1g.**
Sodium **200mg.**

2 large ripe mangoes
1 pineapple, peeled and cut into ¼-inch cubes
¼ cup fresh lime juice
½ cup finely chopped fresh cilantro
1½ lb. medium shrimp, peeled, and deveined if necessary
2 sweet red peppers, halved, seeded and deribbed
¼ cup mayonnaise (recipe, page 13)
4 scallions, trimmed and thinly sliced
2 tbsp. very finely chopped fresh ginger
½ tsp. salt
1 cilantro sprig for garnish

To prepare the relish, first peel the mangoes and remove the flesh in pieces. Purée one quarter of the flesh in a food processor or a blender, then pass it through a sieve set over a bowl. Refrigerate the purée. Cut the remaining mango pieces into ¼-inch cubes and place them in a bowl. Add the pineapple, lime juice and chopped cilantro; stir the relish and refrigerate it.

Bring 2 quarts of water to a boil in a large saucepan. Add the shrimp and cook them until they are opaque — about one minute. Drain the shrimp and refresh them under cold running water. Transfer the shrimp to a bowl.

Dice one of the pepper halves and add the dice to the bowl containing the shrimp. Julienne the remaining pepper halves and set the julienne aside. Stir the mayonnaise, mango purée, scallions, ginger and salt into the shrimp-and-pepper mixture. Chill the salad for at least 30 minutes.

To serve, spoon some of the pineapple-mango relish onto a large platter and surround it with some of the shrimp salad. Top the relish with the remaining shrimp salad; garnish the dish with the pepper julienne and the cilantro sprig.

Mix the scallops and the shrimp with the lemon juice, basil, horseradish and cayenne pepper. Set them aside while you roast the vegetables.

Toss the mushrooms, fennel, celery, carrot, red pepper, green beans, shallots and garlic with the oregano, thyme, salt, olive oil and some black pepper. Spread the vegetables out in a single layer in a large shallow pan and roast them in a preheated 450° oven, stirring frequently, until the shallots are translucent — 10 to 12 minutes. Add the scallops and shrimp, their liquid, and the snow peas; stir to combine all the ingredients and cook them, stirring from time to time, until the seafood is opaque — five to seven minutes. Transfer the mixture to a shallow nonreactive dish to cool at room temperature for 30 minutes.

Arrange the lettuce and endive on a platter or individual plates. Using a slotted spoon, set the vegetables and seafood atop the greens. Pour the liquid left in the dish into a small bowl.

Make the dressing by whisking the lemon juice, Dijon mustard, grainy mustard and yogurt into the reserved liquid. Serve the dressing with the salad.

Oven-Roasted Vegetable Salad with Shrimp and Scallops

Serves 4 as a main course at lunch
Working time: about 45 minutes
Total time: about 1 hour and 15 minutes

Calories **250**
Protein **23g.**
Cholesterol **86mg.**
Total fat **9g.**
Saturated fat **1g.**
Sodium **450mg.**

½ lb. bay scallops, the bright white connective tissue removed
½ lb. medium shrimp, peeled, and deveined if necessary
3 tbsp. fresh lemon juice
1 cup coarsely chopped fresh basil
½ tsp. drained prepared horseradish
¼ tsp. cayenne pepper
½ lb. mushrooms, trimmed and wiped clean
1 small fennel bulb, thinly sliced
2 celery stalks, cut into 2-inch lengths, then into ¼-inch sticks
1 carrot, cut into 2-inch lengths, then into ¼-inch sticks
1 sweet red pepper, seeded, deribbed and cut into thin strips
¼ lb. green beans, trimmed
4 shallots, thinly sliced
1 tbsp. finely chopped garlic
1 tbsp. chopped fresh oregano, or 1 tsp. dried oregano
1 tbsp. fresh thyme, or 1 tsp. dried thyme leaves
½ tsp. salt
2 tbsp. virgin olive oil
freshly ground black pepper
¼ lb. snow peas, stems and strings removed
1 head of green-leaf lettuce, washed and dried
1 head of Belgian endive, leaves separated
¼ cup fresh lemon juice
2 tsp. Dijon mustard
1 tsp. grainy mustard
2 tbsp. plain low-fat yogurt

Clam Salad on Nappa Cabbage

Serves 4 as a main course
Working time: about 1 hour
Total time: about 1 hour and 30 minutes

Calories **235**
Protein **12g.**
Cholesterol **34mg.**
Total fat **8g.**
Saturated fat **1g.**
Sodium **180mg.**

3 scallions, trimmed and finely chopped
1 shallot, finely chopped
1 cup dry sherry
3 tbsp. fresh lemon juice
½ tsp. saffron threads
36 small hard-shell clams, scrubbed
5 round red potatoes or other boiling potatoes
2 tbsp. red wine vinegar
1 tbsp. grainy mustard
freshly ground black pepper
2 tbsp. safflower oil
1 lb. Nappa cabbage, cut into chiffonade (technique, page 51)
2 tbsp. thinly sliced fresh basil, or 2 tsp. dried basil
2 tbsp. finely chopped red onion
½ lb. cherry tomatoes, halved lengthwise

Combine the scallions, shallot, sherry, lemon juice and saffron threads in a large, nonreactive pot. Bring the liquid to a simmer, then reduce the heat to low, cover the mixture, and cook it for one minute.

Add the clams and cover the pot. Increase the heat to medium high and cook the clams, stirring occasionally, until they open — about three minutes. Using a slotted spoon, transfer the clams to a large bowl; discard any clams that remain closed. Strain the clam broth through a sieve lined with cheesecloth into a bowl, taking care not to pour any of the accumulated sand into the sieve. Rinse out the cheesecloth and set it aside. Discard the solids.

When the clams are cool enough to handle, remove them from their shells. Dip each clam into the broth to rinse off any residual sand; reserve the broth. Place the rinsed clams in a bowl, cover the bowl, and refrigerate the clams.

Put the potatoes into a saucepan and pour in enough water to cover them by about 2 inches. Bring the water to a boil and simmer the potatoes until they are tender — about 15 minutes. Drain them and set them aside until they are cool enough to handle.

Cut the potatoes into quarters and transfer them to a nonreactive bowl. Reline the sieve with the cheesecloth and strain the clam broth through it. Pour the strained broth over the potatoes. Gently toss the potatoes and let them stand for 20 minutes.

Remove the potatoes from the broth and set them aside. To prepare the vinaigrette, whisk the vinegar, mustard and some pepper into the broth. Then, whisking constantly, pour in the oil in a thin, steady stream; continue whisking until the oil is fully incorporated.

Toss the cabbage with the basil, onion and about half of the vinaigrette. In a separate bowl, mix the clams and tomatoes with the remaining vinaigrette.

To assemble the salad, spread the cabbage-onion mixture on a platter. Mound the clam-and-tomato mixture in the center and arrange the potatoes around it. Pour any remaining vinaigrette over the potatoes and serve at once.

Crab Meat Salad with Grapes and Jícama

Serves 4 as a main course
Working time: about 1 hour
Total time: about 1 hour and 30 minutes

Calories **220**	¾ lb. crab meat, picked over
Protein **17g.**	½ cup seedless green grapes, halved
Cholesterol **77mg.**	½ cup seedless red grapes, halved
Total fat **8g.**	1 bunch scallions, white parts only, julienned
Saturated fat **1g.**	juice of 1 orange
Sodium **225mg.**	¼ tsp. ground coriander
	¼ tsp. ground cumin
	¼ tsp. ground mace
	¼ tsp. ground ginger
	⅛ tsp. turmeric
	⅛ tsp. white pepper
	¼ cup mayonnaise (recipe, page 13)
	1½ cups jícama julienne
	juice of 1 lemon
	juice of 1 lime
	freshly ground black pepper
	1 navel orange
	6 kumquats (optional), sliced and seeded

In a large bowl, combine the crab meat, green and red grapes, scallions and orange juice. In a small bowl, blend the coriander, cumin, mace, ginger, turmeric and white pepper into the mayonnaise; add this dressing to the crabmeat salad and toss the ingredients well. Refrigerate the salad for at least 30 minutes.

Put the jícama into a third bowl; sprinkle the jícama with the lemon juice, lime juice and a generous grinding of black pepper. Toss the jícama well and chill it for the same length of time as the salad.

Just before serving, cut the orange into segments: Cut away the peel, white pith and outer membrane from the orange. To separate the segments from the inner membranes, slice down to the core with a sharp knife on either side of each segment.

Mound the crab salad and the jícama side by side on a serving platter. Garnish the salad with the orange slices and the kumquats if you are using them, and serve immediately.

Crab Salad with Spinach and Corn

Serves 6 as a main course at lunch
Working time: about 25 minutes
Total time: about 1 hour and 10 minutes
(includes chilling)

Calories **110**	½ lb. fresh spinach, stemmed and washed
Protein **16g.**	1 cup fresh corn kernels (from 1 large ear), or 1 cup frozen corn kernels, defrosted
Cholesterol **59mg.**	1 lb. crab meat, picked over
Total fat **3g.**	1 tomato, peeled, seeded and chopped
Saturated fat **0g.**	2 tbsp. white wine vinegar
Sodium **240mg.**	¼ cup creamy yogurt dressing (recipe, page 13)
	cayenne pepper
	⅛ tsp. salt
	1 head of red-leaf lettuce, washed and dried

Put the spinach, with just the water that clings to its leaves, into a pot. Cover the pot and steam the spinach over medium heat until it wilts — two to three minutes. Drain the spinach; when it is cool enough to handle, squeeze it to remove excess liquid, and chop the spinach coarsely.

If you are using fresh corn, pour enough water into a saucepan to fill it about 1 inch deep. Set a vegetable steamer in the pan and bring the water to a boil. Place the corn in the steamer, cover the pan, and steam the

corn until it is tender — about four minutes. (Frozen corn requires no cooking.)

In a large bowl, combine the spinach, corn, crab meat, tomato and vinegar. Cover the bowl and refrigerate it for at least 30 minutes.

Shortly before assembling the salad, whisk together the yogurt dressing, a pinch of cayenne pepper and the salt. Pour the dressing over the salad and toss well. Arrange the lettuce leaves on a serving platter. Mound the salad on the leaves and serve immediately.

Squid Salad with Scallions and Crushed Coriander

Serves 4 as a main course
Working time: about 25 minutes
Total time: about 1 hour

Calories **175**
Protein **16g.**
Cholesterol **223mg.**
Total fat **8g.**
Saturated fat **1g.**
Sodium **400mg.**

1 ¼ lb. small squid, cleaned and peeled, the tentacles reserved
2 tbsp. virgin olive oil
¼ tsp. salt
freshly ground black pepper
1 tsp. coriander seeds, crushed
2 tbsp. sherry vinegar
1 tbsp. fresh lemon juice
½ sweet red pepper, seeded, deribbed and diced
½ yellow pepper, seeded, deribbed and diced
4 scallions, trimmed and sliced diagonally into thin ovals
1 head of Boston lettuce, or 2 heads of Bibb lettuce, washed and dried
lemon slices for garnish

Slice the squid pouches into thin rings.

Heat 1 tablespoon of the olive oil in a large, heavy-bottomed skillet over high heat. When the oil is hot, add the squid rings and tentacles, ⅛ teaspoon of the salt and some pepper. Sauté the squid, stirring constantly, until it turns opaque — about two minutes. Drain the squid well, reserving the cooking juices, and transfer the squid pieces to a large bowl; put the bowl in the refrigerator.

Pour the cooking juices into a small saucepan; add the crushed coriander and boil the liquid until only 2 tablespoons remain — about three minutes. Remove the pan from the heat, then whisk in the vinegar, lemon juice, the remaining ⅛ teaspoon of salt and the remaining tablespoon of oil. Pour this dressing over the squid; add the peppers and scallions, and toss the mixture. Chill the salad for at least 30 minutes.

Just before serving the salad, grind in a generous amount of black pepper and toss the ingredients well. Present the salad on the lettuce leaves, garnished with lemon slices.

Clam and Corn Salad

Serves 6 as a main course at lunch
Working time: about 45 minutes
Total time: about 1 hour and 15 minutes

Calories **150**
Protein **9g.**
Cholesterol **23mg.**
Total fat **8g.**
Saturated fat **1g.**
Sodium **100mg.**

5 scallions, trimmed and finely chopped
1 garlic clove, finely chopped
1 cup dry white wine
¼ cup fresh lemon juice
36 small hard-shell clams, scrubbed
½ lb. mushrooms, wiped clean, stemmed and quartered
3 carrots, cut diagonally into ¼-inch-thick slices
3 celery stalks, trimmed and cut diagonally into ¼-inch-thick slices
2 cups fresh corn kernels (from about 2 large ears), or 2 cups frozen corn, defrosted
1 tbsp. chopped fresh parsley
1 tbsp. white wine vinegar
freshly ground black pepper
2 tbsp. virgin olive oil
1 lb. fresh spinach, washed, stemmed and cut into chiffonade (technique, page 51)

Combine the scallions, garlic, wine and 3 tablespoons of the lemon juice in a large pot. Bring the mixture to a boil. Add the clams to the boiling liquid. Cover the pot and cook the clams until they open — about three minutes. Using a slotted spoon, transfer the clams to a large bowl; discard any clams that remain closed. Strain the broth through a sieve lined with cheesecloth into a bowl, taking care not to pour any of the accumulated sand into the sieve.

When the clams are cool enough to handle, remove them from their shells. Dip each clam into the broth to rinse off any residual sand. Transfer the rinsed clams to a bowl; cover the bowl and refrigerate it.

Strain the clam broth once more and pour it into a saucepan. Add the mushrooms and the remaining tablespoon of lemon juice to the saucepan. Bring the broth to a boil, then reduce the heat, cover the pan and simmer the mushrooms for two minutes. With a slotted spoon, transfer the mushrooms to a bowl.

Add the carrots and celery to the clam broth in the saucepan; cover the pan and simmer the vegetables for three minutes. Using a slotted spoon, add the carrots and celery to the mushrooms; do not discard the broth. Let the vegetables cool to room temperature.

If you are using fresh corn, pour enough water into a saucepan to fill it about 1 inch deep. Set a steamer in the saucepan and put the corn into the steamer. Bring the water to a boil, tightly cover the pan, and steam the corn for three minutes. (Frozen corn requires no steaming.)

To prepare the dressing, whisk the parsley, vinegar, some pepper and the oil into the reserved clam broth. Add all the vegetables to the bowl containing the clams; pour about ¾ of the dressing over the salad and toss it well.

Arrange the spinach chiffonade on individual plates. Spoon some of the salad onto each plate; pass the remaining dressing separately.

Mussel and Sprouted Lentil Salad

Serves 6 as a main course at lunch
Working time: about 35 minutes
Total time: about 1 hour (includes chilling)

Calories **120**
Protein **9g.**
Cholesterol **27mg.**
Total fat **4g.**
Saturated fat **0g.**
Sodium **225mg.**

36 mussels, scrubbed and debearded
2 carrots, julienned
¼ tsp. salt
freshly ground black pepper
2 tbsp. white wine vinegar
1 tbsp. safflower oil
1 garlic clove, finely chopped
1 lb. ripe tomatoes peeled, seeded and coarsely chopped, or 14 oz. canned unsalted tomatoes, drained and coarsely chopped
1 tbsp. fennel seeds
2 cups sprouted lentils (instructions, page 37)
1 head of green-leaf lettuce, washed and dried

Bring ½ cup of water to a boil in a large pot; add the mussels and cover the pot. Steam the mussels until they open — about three minutes. With a slotted spoon, remove the mussels and set them aside; discard any that remain closed. Strain the cooking liquid through a sieve lined with doubled cheesecloth, taking care not to pour any of the sand into the sieve. Reserve the liquid.

When the mussels are cool enough to handle, re-

move them from their shells. Dip each mussel into the reserved liquid to rinse away any residual sand. Put the rinsed mussels into a large bowl. Reline the sieve with cheesecloth and strain the liquid through it again; set the liquid aside.

Bring 6 cups of water to a boil in a saucepan. Add the carrots and blanch them for two minutes, then refresh them under cold running water. Drain the carrots well, add them to the mussels, and season with the salt, some pepper and the vinegar.

Heat the oil in a heavy-bottomed saucepan over medium heat; add the garlic and sauté it for one minute. Add the tomatoes, the fennel seeds and ½ cup of the reserved mussel liquid; increase the heat to medium high and bring the liquid to a boil. Reduce the heat to maintain a strong simmer and cook the tomato mixture until nearly all the liquid has evaporated — about five minutes.

Meanwhile, blanch the lentil sprouts in 6 cups of boiling water for three minutes. Drain the sprouts, refresh them under cold running water, and drain them again. Add the sprouts and the tomato mixture to the mussels and toss well. Refrigerate the salad for one hour before presenting it on a bed of lettuce.

Mussel Salad

Serves 4 as a first course
Working time: about 30 minutes
Total time: about 1 hour

Calories **175**	½ cup rice
Protein **7g.**	1 tbsp. fennel seeds
Cholesterol **27mg.**	2 tbsp. finely chopped green pepper
Total fat **5g.**	¼ cup finely chopped red onion
Saturated fat **1g.**	1 small ripe tomato, peeled, seeded and chopped
Sodium **125mg.**	1 small garlic clove, finely chopped
	1 tbsp. prepared horseradish, drained
	3 tbsp. white wine vinegar
	24 mussels, scrubbed and debearded
	1 tbsp. virgin olive oil
	fresh parsley sprigs for garnish

Put the rice, the fennel seeds and 1 cup of water into a small saucepan over medium-high heat. Bring the water to a boil, then reduce the heat, cover the pot, and simmer the rice until it is tender — 20 to 25 minutes. Set the rice aside.

While the rice is simmering, prepare the marinade. In a nonreactive bowl, mix together the green pepper, onion, tomato, garlic, horseradish and vinegar. Set the marinade aside while you cook the mussels.

Bring 1 cup of water to a boil in a large pot. Add the mussels and cover the pot. Steam the mussels until they open — two to three minutes. Discard any mussels that remain closed. Strain the cooking liquid through a sieve lined with doubled cheesecloth, tak-

ing care not to pour any of the sand into the sieve. Reserve the liquid.

Using a slotted spoon, transfer the mussels to a large bowl. When the mussels are cool enough to handle, remove them from their shells, reserving one half of each shell. Dip each mussel into the reserved liquid to rinse away any residual sand. Pat the mussels dry, then add them to the marinade, and let them stand at room temperature for 30 minutes.

Stir the rice and oil into the marinated mussels. Fill each reserved mussel shell with one mussel and about 2 teaspoons of the rice-and-vegetable mixture. Arrange the stuffed shells on a platter; garnish the platter with the parsley just before serving.

Turkey Salad with Green and Red Grapes

Serves 4 as a main course
Working time: about 20 minutes
Total time: about 1 hour and 30 minutes

Calories **290**
Protein **27g.**
Cholesterol **59mg.**
Total fat **17g.**
Saturated fat **2g.**
Sodium **200mg.**

1 lb. skinless turkey breast meat
2 tbsp. fresh lemon juice
1 tbsp. virgin olive oil
1 tbsp. fresh thyme, or 1 tsp. dried thyme leaves
⅛ tsp. salt
freshly ground black pepper
2 tbsp. sliced almonds
½ cup seedless green grapes
½ cup seedless red grapes
3 scallions, trimmed and thinly sliced
¼ cup vinaigrette (recipe, page 13)
1 small head of red-leaf lettuce, washed and dried

Preheat the oven to 375° F.

Put the turkey meat in a small baking dish and sprin-kle it with the lemon juice, oil, thyme, salt and some pepper. Rub the seasonings into the meat and let it marinate at room temperature for 20 minutes.

At the end of the marinating time, roast the meat, turning it once, until it feels firm but springy to the touch — about 20 minutes.

While the meat is cooking, spread the almonds on a small baking sheet or ovenproof skillet and toast them in the oven until they are golden brown — about four minutes. Set the almonds aside.

When the turkey has finished cooking, remove it from the oven and let it cool in the dish. As soon as the meat is cool enough to handle, remove it from the dish and cut it diagonally into thin slices. Lay the slices in the pan juices and refrigerate them for at least 30 minutes.

To assemble the salad, combine the grapes, scallions and vinaigrette in a bowl. Arrange the turkey slices on the lettuce leaves and mound the grape-scallion mix-ture on top; sprinkle the salad with the toasted al-monds and serve immediately.

Turkey and Peach Roses

Serves 6 as a main course
Working time: about 30 minutes
Total time: about 1 hour and 30 minutes

Calories **225**
Protein **27g.**
Cholesterol **59mg.**
Total fat **10g.**
Saturated fat **2g.**
Sodium **150mg.**

1 skinned and boned turkey breast half (about 1½ lb.)
¼ tsp. salt
3 tbsp. fresh orange juice
1½ tbsp. red wine vinegar
¼ tsp. Dijon mustard
freshly ground black pepper
1½ tbsp. safflower oil
1½ tbsp. virgin olive oil
3 large ripe peaches, the fuzz wiped away with a cloth
1 head of red-leaf lettuce, washed and dried
3 tbsp. small basil or cilantro leaves

Sprinkle the turkey breast with ⅛ teaspoon of the salt. Enclose the breast tightly in three layers of plastic wrap, creating a long waterproof package. Pour enough water into a large, deep skillet or pot to fill it about 3 inches deep. Bring the water to the barest simmer and add the breast. Cook the meat for 20 minutes, maintaining a simmer throughout the cooking; do not let the water come to a boil. Turn the turkey over and continue cooking it for 10 minutes more. Remove the turkey from the water and transfer it, still wrapped in plastic, to the refrigerator.

To make the vinaigrette, combine the orange juice, vinegar, mustard, some pepper and the remaining ⅛ teaspoon of salt in a small bowl. Whisking vigorously, pour in the safflower oil in a thin, steady stream; incorporate the olive oil the same way.

Cut the peaches in half, then cut each half into thin wedges; you will need 42 slices. Place the slices in a small bowl and spoon 3 tablespoons of the vinaigrette over them. Put the bowl in the refrigerator.

When the turkey breast is cool, remove the plastic wrap and cut the meat against the grain into ¼-inch-thick slices; you will need 36 slices.

Line six salad plates with the lettuce leaves. To fashion the roses, first arrange three peach wedges in a loose circle on one of the plates. Place two larger turkey slices inside the circle, nestling them within the curve of the peaches and tucking their ends in. Next arrange two peach wedges inside the circle, facing each other. Build another layer using two medium slices of turkey and two peach slices. To form the flower's center, roll up a small turkey slice and insert it between the peaches; tightly roll up a final small slice of turkey and tuck it in the center of the rose. Repeat the process to form five more roses from the remaining peach wedges and turkey slices. Drizzle the remaining vinaigrette over the roses and garnish them with the basil or cilantro leaves; serve immediately.

the bowl and marinate the chicken for two hours in the refrigerator.

At the end of the marinating period, remove the thighs from the liquid and pat them dry with paper towels. Reserve the marinade. Heat the oil in a large, heavy-bottomed pot over medium heat. Add the thighs and cook them until they are browned on all sides — about 10 minutes. Stir in the barley, the stock and ½ cup of the reserved marinade. Bring the liquid to a boil, reduce the heat, and simmer the mixture until the barley is tender and most of the liquid has evaporated — about 30 minutes.

Remove the thighs and set them aside; when they are cool enough to handle, pull the meat from the bones and chop it coarsely. Add the chicken to the barley, then add the parsley, the remaining mint and the remaining 2 tablespoons of lemon juice. Mix the salad well and serve it on a bed of iceberg lettuce, garnished with the mint sprigs.

Chicken Salad
with Barley and Mint

Serves 6 as a main course
Working time: about 45 minutes
Total time: about 3 hours and 20 minutes
(includes marinating)

Calories **410**
Protein **30g.**
Cholesterol **81mg.**
Total fat **15g.**
Saturated fat **3g.**
Sodium **320mg.**

2 lb. chicken thighs, skinned and trimmed of fat
½ cup plus 2 tbsp. fresh lemon juice
½ tsp. ground cumin
½ tsp. dry mustard
½ tsp. paprika
½ tsp. ground cinnamon
½ tsp. cayenne pepper
½ tsp. salt
freshly ground black pepper
3 tbsp. chopped fresh mint, or 1 tbsp. dried mint
1 garlic clove, finely chopped
2 tbsp. safflower oil
1⅓ cups pearl barley
4 cups unsalted chicken stock
1 tbsp. chopped fresh parsley, preferably Italian
1 small head of iceberg lettuce
several mint sprigs

Put the chicken thighs in a large bowl. In a smaller bowl, combine ½ cup of the lemon juice, the cumin, mustard, paprika, cinnamon, cayenne pepper, salt, some black pepper, 1 tablespoon of the fresh mint or 1 teaspoon dried mint, and the garlic. Pour this marinade over the thighs, and stir to coat them. Cover

Chicken and Avocado
Salad with
Tomatillo Sauce

Serves 4 as a main course
Working time: about 25 minutes
Total time: about 45 minutes

Calories **310**
Protein **29g.**
Cholesterol **72mg.**
Total fat **18g.**
Saturated fat **3g.**
Sodium **215mg.**

1 tsp. safflower oil
4 chicken breast halves, skinned and boned (about 1 lb.)
¼ tsp. salt
freshly ground black pepper
⅓ lb. tomatillos, husked and washed
1½ tbsp. virgin olive oil
¼ cup chopped onion
1 garlic clove, thinly sliced
1½ tbsp. fresh lemon juice
5 fresh basil leaves, thinly sliced
1 head of radicchio or red-leaf lettuce, washed and dried
1 ripe avocado, peeled, pitted and rubbed with 1 tbsp. fresh lemon juice
1 tomato, seeded and finely chopped

Heat the safflower oil in a large, heavy-bottomed skillet over very low heat. Sprinkle the chicken breasts with ⅛ teaspoon of the salt and some pepper, and place them in the skillet. Set a heavy plate atop the chicken breasts to weight them down so that they will cook evenly. Cook the breasts on one side for five minutes; turn them over, cover them with the plate, and cook the breasts for three to four minutes more. The meat should feel firm but springy to the touch, with no traces of pink along the edges. Transfer the chicken breasts to a plate and refrigerate them while you finish the salad.

Finely dice two of the tomatillos and set the pieces aside; cut the remaining tomatillos into quarters. Heat the olive oil in the skillet over medium heat, then add the onion and garlic, and cook them for two minutes. Stir in the tomatillo quarters, the lemon juice, basil and the remaining ⅛ teaspoon of salt. Cook the mixture, stirring often, until the tomatillos are soft — about seven minutes. Transfer the contents of the skillet to a food processor or blender and purée the mixture. Pour the sauce into a bowl and stir in the diced tomatillos. Chill the sauce for at least 20 minutes.

Arrange a few radicchio or lettuce leaves on four plates. Slice the breasts diagonally and fan out each one on the leaves. Cut the avocado into thin slices and tuck them between the chicken slices. Spoon a large dollop of the tomatillo sauce onto the base of each fan, then sprinkle chopped tomato over the sauce. Grind fresh pepper over all, if you wish, and serve.

Curried Chicken Salad with Raisins

Serves 6 as a main course
Working time: about 20 minutes
Total time: about 1 hour

Calories **250**
Protein **20g.**
Cholesterol **55mg.**
Total fat **9g.**
Saturated fat **2g.**
Sodium **190mg.**

1 tsp. safflower oil
6 chicken breast halves, skinned and boned (about 1 ½ lb.)
¼ tsp. salt
½ cup raisins
1 large carrot, grated
1 onion, grated
1 celery stalk, chopped
3 tbsp. fresh lemon juice
1 tbsp. curry powder
1 tbsp. honey
¼ cup mayonnaise (recipe, page 13)
¾ cup julienned radish
½ tbsp. virgin olive oil
1 small head of romaine lettuce, washed and dried
2 ripe tomatoes, cored and sliced into wedges

Heat the safflower oil in a large, heavy-bottomed skillet over low heat. Sprinkle the chicken breasts with the salt and place them in the skillet. Set a heavy plate atop the chicken breasts to weight them down so that they will cook evenly. Cook the breasts on the first side for five minutes; turn them over, weight them down again with the plate, and cook them on the second side for three to four minutes. The meat should feel firm but springy to the touch, with no traces of pink along the edges. Transfer the breasts to a plate and chill them. When the chicken is cool enough to handle, cut it into 1-inch cubes.

In a large mixing bowl, toss the chicken cubes with the raisins, carrot, onion, celery, lemon juice, curry powder, honey and mayonnaise. Chill the salad for at least 30 minutes.

Toss the radish julienne with the olive oil in a small bowl. Mound the chicken salad on the lettuce leaves, and garnish each plate with the radish julienne and the tomato wedges. Serve immediately

Salad of Broiled Quail with Dried Fruits

Serves 4 as a main course
Working time: about 45 minutes
Total time: about 2 hours and 30 minutes
(includes marinating)

Calories **480**
Protein **25g.**
Cholesterol **87mg.**
Total fat **22g.**
Saturated fat **4g.**
Sodium **300mg.**

4 quail
2 scallions, trimmed and finely chopped
2 garlic cloves, finely chopped
2 tbsp. safflower oil
6 tbsp. Armagnac or brandy
¼ tsp. salt
1 tsp. fresh thyme, or ¼ tsp. dried thyme leaves
1 tsp. chili powder
¼ cup golden raisins
¼ cup dark raisins
¼ cup currants
¼ cup sliced dried apricots
2 tbsp. sugar
1 tbsp. grated orange zest
1 cup unsalted chicken stock
¼ cup fresh lemon juice
1 tbsp. grainy mustard
½ lb. fresh spinach, washed, stemmed and dried
1 oz. fresh sorrel (optional), washed, stemmed and dried

Lay a quail breast side down on a cutting board. To halve the bird, cut through the back, from neck to tail, along one side of the backbone. Spread the quail open and cut through the center of the breastbone from neck to tail. Halve the remaining quail the same way. Put the quail halves into a baking dish large enough to accommodate them in a single layer.

Whisk together the scallions, garlic, 1 tablespoon of the oil, 2 tablespoons of the Armagnac or brandy, the salt, thyme and chili powder. Pour this marinade over the quail halves and turn them once or twice in the liquid to coat them evenly. Cover the dish and refrigerate it for two hours.

About halfway through the marinating period, prepare the dried fruits. Put the golden raisins, dark raisins, currants, apricots, sugar and orange zest into a saucepan. Pour in enough water to cover the fruits by about ½ inch. Bring the liquid to a boil, then reduce the heat, and simmer the fruits for five minutes. Pour in the stock, the lemon juice, and the remaining 2 tablespoons of Armagnac or brandy, and simmer the liquid until it is reduced by one half — about 40 minutes. Strain the fruits, reserving their cooking liquid.

When the quail finish marinating, broil them in their baking dish for five to seven minutes per side. While the quail are cooking, assemble the remaining components of the salad. Put the spinach and the sorrel, if you are using it, into a large bowl. In a small bowl, whisk together the reserved cooking liquid, the remaining tablespoon of oil and the mustard. Pour half of this dressing over the greens and toss well.

Arrange the dressed greens on individual plates and top them with the fruits. Set two quail halves on each plate; pour the remaining dressing over all and serve.

Chicken and Grapefruit Salad

Serves 6 as a main course
Working time: about 1 hour and 15 minutes
Total time: about 3 hours and 30 minutes
(includes marinating)

Calories **350**
Protein **26g.**
Cholesterol **80mg.**
Total fat **13g.**
Saturated fat **3g.**
Sodium **300mg.**

2 lb. chicken thighs, skinned and trimmed of fat
⅔ cup dry vermouth
½ tsp. salt
1 tbsp. chopped fresh oregano, or 1 tsp. dried oregano
1 tsp. anise seeds
2 garlic cloves, finely chopped
1 shallot, finely chopped
3 tbsp. honey
freshly ground black pepper
2 tbsp. virgin olive oil
4 carrots, quartered lengthwise and cut into 1-inch lengths
4 celery stalks, halved lengthwise and cut into 1-inch lengths
½ cup unsalted chicken stock
4 grapefruits
1 bunch of watercress, trimmed, washed and dried

Put the chicken thighs into a bowl with the vermouth, salt, oregano, anise seeds, garlic, shallot, 2 tablespoons of the honey and some pepper. Stir to combine the ingredients, then cover the bowl and let the chicken marinate in the refrigerator for two hours.

At the end of the marinating period, preheat the oven to 375° F. Drain the chicken and pat it dry with paper towels. Strain the marinade, reserving both liquid and solids. Heat the oil in a heavy-bottomed oven-proof pot over medium-high heat. Add the chicken thighs to the pot and sauté them until they are browned on all sides — about 10 minutes. Remove the thighs from the pot. Add the reserved solids to the pot and sauté them for one minute. Add the carrots and celery, then pour in the stock, and simmer the mixture for two minutes.

Set the chicken thighs atop the vegetables in the pot and transfer the pot, uncovered, to the oven. Bake the chicken and vegetables, stirring occasionally, until the juices run clear from a thigh pierced with a knife — about 25 minutes.

Remove the chicken from the pot and set it aside to cool. Then remove the vegetables and set them aside to cool as well.

While the chicken and vegetables are cooling, prepare the grapefruits and the dressing. Cut away the peel and pith from a grapefruit. To separate the segments from the inner membranes, slice down to the core on either side of each segment, working over a bowl to catch the juice. Discard the seeds and set the segments aside as you go. Squeeze the pulpy core of membranes over the bowl to extract every bit of juice. Repeat the process to segment the remaining three grapefruits.

Pour the reserved marinade into a small saucepan. Add the grapefruit juice and the remaining tablespoon of honey. Bring the liquid to a boil and cook it until it is reduced to about ⅔ cup — five to 10 minutes.

When the chicken is cool enough to handle, pull the meat from the bones and cut it into thin strips. Arrange the watercress on a platter. Top it with the vegetables, then with a layer of the grapefruit segments. Scatter the chicken on top of the grapefruit; just before serving the salad, pour the reduced marinade over all.

Lamb Salad with Fig Sauce

Serves 8 as a main course
Working time: about 35 minutes
Total time: about 2 hours

Calories **385**	
Protein **24g.**	*1 tbsp. safflower oil*
Cholesterol **60mg.**	*one 3-lb. leg of lamb shank half, trimmed of fat*
Total fat **22g.**	*¼ tsp. salt*
Saturated fat **10g.**	*freshly ground black pepper*
Sodium **155mg.**	*2 tbsp. virgin olive oil*
	1¼ cups quartered, dried Calimyrna figs (about 6 oz.)
	¼ cup chopped shallot
	½ tbsp. fresh thyme, or ½ tsp. dried thyme leaves
	1 cup unsalted veal or chicken stock
	5 tbsp. sherry vinegar or red wine vinegar
	1 large head of escarole (about 1½ lb.), washed and dried
	several thyme sprigs for garnish (optional)

Preheat the oven to 350° F. Heat the safflower oil in a large ovenproof skillet over medium-high heat. Add the lamb and brown it well on all sides — 10 to 12 minutes. Sprinkle the lamb with the salt and some pepper, then transfer the skillet to the oven. If you like your meat medium rare, roast the lamb for about one hour; if you prefer it medium, roast the lamb for an hour and 15 minutes. Remove the lamb from the skillet and set it aside to cool.

Return the skillet to the stove, setting it over medium heat. Add 1 tablespoon of the olive oil, the figs, shallot, thyme and some pepper. Cook the mixture, stirring frequently, for three minutes. Pour in the stock and ¼ cup of the vinegar. Reduce the heat to low and simmer the mixture, stirring occasionally, for five minutes.

Remove 16 fig quarters from the skillet and set them aside. To make the sauce, transfer the remaining contents of the skillet to a food processor or a blender. Purée the mixture, scraping down the sides at least once during the process. Transfer the sauce to a bowl and chill it.

When the lamb has cooled, slice it thinly against the grain. Toss the escarole with the remaining tablespoon of olive oil, the remaining tablespoon of vinegar and a generous grinding of pepper.

Spread the escarole on individual salad plates and arrange the lamb slices on top. Pour the fig sauce over the lamb; garnish the salads with the reserved fig quarters and the thyme sprigs, and serve immediately.

Lamb Salad with Marinated Eggplant

Serves 6 as a main course
Working time: about 50 minutes
Total time: about 3 hours (includes marinating)

Calories **305**
Protein **23g.**
Cholesterol **53mg.**
Total fat **18g.**
Saturated fat **9g.**
Sodium **155mg.**

one 1½-lb. boneless leg of lamb, trimmed of fat
1½ tsp. chopped fresh rosemary, or ½ tsp. dried rosemary, crumbled
1 small red onion, chopped
freshly ground black pepper
3 tbsp. red wine
3 tbsp. red wine vinegar
1 eggplant (about 1 lb.), quartered lengthwise and thinly sliced
½ tsp. salt
1 tbsp. fresh thyme, or 1 tsp. dried thyme leaves
1 tsp. chopped fresh parsley
1 tbsp. olive oil
2 tbsp. balsamic vinegar, or 1½ tbsp. red wine vinegar mixed with ½ tsp. honey
3 tbsp. tomato paste
2 ripe tomatoes (about 1 lb.), peeled, seeded and chopped
1 bunch of watercress, washed, stemmed and dried

Lay the leg of lamb in a shallow, nonreactive dish. Scatter the rosemary and onion over the meat, then season it with some pepper, and pour in the wine and wine vinegar. Turn the meat to moisten both sides.

Cover the dish and marinate the lamb in the refrigerator for two hours.

Toss the eggplant slices with the salt and drain them in a colander for one hour.

Preheat the oven to 450° F. Rinse the eggplant slices and pat them dry, then transfer them to a roasting pan. Sprinkle the thyme and parsley over the slices; drizzle the oil over the top. Roast the eggplant, stirring frequently, until it is tender — about 25 minutes.

Transfer the roasted eggplant to a bowl. Whisk together the balsamic vinegar or wine vinegar mixed with honey, and 2 tablespoons of the tomato paste. Pour this mixture over the eggplant, mix well and set the bowl aside.

Remove the lamb and pat it dry. Reserve the marinade for the dressing. Put the lamb in a roasting pan and roast it until it is medium rare — about one hour. Transfer the lamb to a cutting board and let it rest.

To make the dressing, pour the reserved marinade into the roasting pan. Set the pan on the stove and bring the liquid to a boil, scraping with a wooden spoon to dissolve the pan deposits. Strain the liquid into a small bowl, then stir in the chopped tomatoes and the remaining tablespoon of tomato paste; set the dressing aside.

Slice the lamb and arrange it on a platter with the watercress and the eggplant. Pour some of the dressing over the lamb and present the rest alongside.

Pork, Nectarine and Orange Salad

Serves 4 as a main course
Working time: about 40 minutes
Total time: about 1 hour and 10 minutes

Calories **310**
Protein **27g.**
Cholesterol **79mg.**
Total fat **12g.**
Saturated fat **2g.**
Sodium **250mg.**

½ tsp. ground ginger
½ tsp. dry mustard
½ tsp. ground coriander
¼ tsp. cayenne pepper
¼ tsp. salt
1 lb. pork tenderloin, trimmed of fat
2 tbsp. safflower oil
3 navel oranges
3 tbsp. sherry vinegar
1 tbsp. chopped fresh cilantro
3 nectarines, cut into wedges
1 bunch of young beet greens, or ¼ lb. spinach, washed, stemmed and dried

Preheat the oven to 400° F.

Combine the ginger, mustard, coriander, cayenne pepper and salt in a small bowl. Rub this mixture into the pork with your hands.

Heat ½ tablespoon of the oil in a large, ovenproof skillet over medium-high heat. Add the pork and sauté it until it is well browned on all sides — five to six minutes. Transfer the skillet to the oven and roast the pork until it feels firm to the touch and the juices run clear when it is pierced with a skewer — 20 to 25 minutes. Remove the pork from the skillet and let it cool to room temperature — about 20 minutes.

While the pork is roasting, prepare the oranges. First cut away the peel and the white pith below it. Then, to separate the orange segments from the internal membranes, slice down to the core on either side of each segment, holding the fruit over a bowl to catch the juice. Set the segments aside as you go.

Drain off any fat in the skillet and return the skillet to the stove over medium-high heat. Pour in the vinegar and the orange juice; bring the liquid to a boil, scraping constantly with a wooden spoon to dissolve any caramelized juices. Strain the liquid into a large bowl; whisk in the cilantro and the remaining 1½ tablespoons of oil, then add the orange and nectarine pieces, and toss the mixture well.

With a slotted spoon, transfer the fruit to a plate lined with the beet greens or spinach. Slice the pork thinly and arrange the slices with the fruit. Pour the dressing remaining in the bowl over all. Serve at once.

Pork and Clam Salad

Serves 6 as a main course
Working time: about 1 hour and 30 minutes
Total time: about 3 hours and 15 minutes
(includes chilling)

Calories **425**
Protein **27g.**
Cholesterol **76mg.**
Total fat **9g.**
Saturated fat **2g.**
Sodium **290mg.**

1 lb. boneless pork loin, trimmed of fat and cut into ½-inch cubes
1 cup dry white wine
2 tbsp. fresh lemon juice
½ tsp. salt
freshly ground black pepper
¼ tsp. cayenne pepper
2 tbsp. chopped fresh cilantro
4 garlic cloves, finely chopped
2 tbsp. virgin olive oil
1 shallot, finely chopped
36 small hard-shell clams, scrubbed
1 small red onion, thinly sliced
1 small sweet red pepper, seeded, deribbed and cut into short, thin strips
1 small green pepper, seeded, deribbed and cut into short, thin strips
4 ripe tomatoes, peeled, seeded and julienned
1½ cups long-grain rice
2 cups unsalted chicken stock
1 bunch of watercress, trimmed, washed and dried

Combine the pork, wine, 1 tablespoon of the lemon juice, the salt, some black pepper, the cayenne pepper, 1 tablespoon of the cilantro and half of the garlic in a nonreactive bowl. Cover the bowl and refrigerate it for two hours.

Heat 1 tablespoon of the olive oil in a large pot over medium-high heat. Add the shallot and the remaining garlic, and sauté them for one minute. Put the clams into the pot. Cover the pot and cook the clams, stirring occasionally, until they open — three to five minutes. Using a slotted spoon, transfer the clams to a large bowl; discard any clams that remain closed. Strain the cooking liquid through a sieve lined with cheesecloth, taking care not to pour into the sieve any of the accumulated sand from the pot. Discard the solids.

When the clams are cool enough to handle, remove them from their shells, then dip them one at a time into the strained cooking liquid to rinse off any residual grains of sand. Transfer the rinsed clams to a bowl. Rinse out the cheesecloth and reline the sieve with it. Strain the broth again and pour it over the clams. ▶

Add to the clams the remaining tablespoon of lemon juice, the onion, red pepper, green pepper, tomatoes and the remaining cilantro; toss the mixture well, then cover the bowl and refrigerate it.

Remove the pork from the marinade, reserving the marinade; pat the meat dry. Heat the remaining tablespoon of oil in a heavy-bottomed pot over medium-high heat. Add the pork loin and sauté it until it is browned — about five minutes.

Add the rice, stock and reserved marinade to the pot. Bring the liquid to a boil, then reduce the heat and simmer the mixture, covered, until the rice has absorbed all the liquid and is tender — 18 to 20 minutes. Remove the pork and rice from the pot and spread it in a flat pan; when it is cool, mix it with the clams and vegetables. Serve the salad on a bed of watercress.

Shredded Beef Salad with Marinated Carrot Strips

Serves 8 as a main course
Working time: about 45 minutes
Total time: about 4 hours

Calories **255**
Protein **27g.**
Cholesterol **77mg.**
Total fat **12g.**
Saturated fat **4g.**
Sodium **190mg.**

3 tbsp. safflower oil
2 lb. lean beef chuck, trimmed of fat
6 medium carrots
1 cup unsalted veal or chicken stock
2 onions, coarsely chopped
3 garlic cloves, crushed
1 tbsp. fresh thyme, or 1 tsp. dried thyme leaves
3 bay leaves, crumbled
1 tsp. sugar
½ cup cider vinegar
¼ tsp. salt
2 tbsp. hoisin sauce
freshly ground black pepper
several Nappa cabbage or escarole leaves, washed and dried
4 scallions (optional), cut into brushes and soaked in ice water

Heat 1 tablespoon of the safflower oil in a large, heavy-bottomed skillet over medium-high heat. Add the beef and sear it in the oil until it is well browned on all sides — about 10 minutes.

Slice one of the carrots into thin rounds and add it to the skillet along with the stock, onions, garlic, thyme and bay leaves. Pour in enough water to raise the depth of the liquid in the skillet to about 1 inch. Bring the liquid to a simmer, then reduce the heat to low; partially cover the skillet and cook the beef slowly until it is quite tender — about three hours. If the liquid falls below ¼ inch during the cooking, add another ½ cup of water to the skillet.

While the meat is cooking, use a vegetable peeler to pare long, thin strips from the outside of the remaining five carrots; discard the woody cores. Put the strips into a large bowl with the sugar and all but 2 tablespoons of the vinegar; toss well. Set the carrot strips aside to marinate, stirring them from time to time.

When the beef is tender, remove it from the skillet and set it aside. Strain the cooking liquid; pour half of it into a small saucepan and discard the rest. Rapidly boil the liquid until only ¼ cup remains. Skim any fat from the surface and set the liquid aside.

When the beef is cool enough to handle, shred it with your fingers, discarding any fat. Heat 1 tablespoon of the remaining oil in the skillet over medium-high heat. Add the beef and the salt; sauté the beef, stirring constantly, for one minute. Pour in the reduced cooking liquid, the remaining 2 tablespoons of vinegar and the hoisin sauce; sprinkle in some pepper and cook the beef for one minute more, stirring all the while. Transfer the beef to a bowl and chill it.

Rinse out and dry the skillet, then return it to the stove over medium-high heat. Pour in the remaining tablespoon of oil; when it is hot, add the carrot strips and their marinade. Sauté the strips, stirring constantly, until all the liquid has evaporated — one or two minutes. Transfer the carrot strips to a bowl and chill them for 30 minutes.

To serve the salad, arrange the cabbage or escarole leaves on a large plate; scatter the carrot strips on top, mound the beef in the center and garnish with the scallions if you are using them.

Pot-au-Feu Salad

Serves 4 as a main course
Working time: about 50 minutes
Total time: about 5 hours and 30 minutes
(includes chilling)

Calories **510**
Protein **33g.**
Cholesterol **101mg.**
Total fat **23g.**
Saturated fat **5g.**
Sodium **400mg.**

½ tbsp. safflower oil
1 lb. boneless beef chuck, trimmed of fat
1 calf's foot or 2 fresh pig's feet
¼ tsp. salt
8 cups unsalted veal or chicken stock
4 carrots, cut into 2-inch segments, each segment quartered lengthwise
2 turnips, peeled, each cut into wedges
4 leeks, trimmed, split lengthwise and washed thoroughly to remove all grit
4 small round red potatoes, each cut into wedges
2 tbsp. chopped parsley
1 head of green-leaf lettuce, washed and dried
½ cup mayonnaise (recipe, page 13)

Heat the safflower oil in a large, heavy-bottomed pot over medium-high heat. Add the beef and brown it on all sides — about 10 minutes. Next add the calf's foot or pig's feet, the salt and the stock; bring the liquid to a simmer and cook it for one and a half hours. Strain and reserve the broth. Reserve the beef; discard the other solids.

Rinse out the pot and return the beef and broth to it. Add the carrots, turnips, leeks and potatoes, and bring the liquid to a boil. Reduce the heat to low and simmer the pot-au-feu until all the ingredients are tender — about 35 minutes. Remove the pot from the heat and let the contents cool to room temperature — about 30 minutes. Spoon the fat from the surface, then blot any remaining traces with a paper towel. Remove the beef and vegetables from the broth and set them aside in the refrigerator. Pour 2 cups of the broth into a bowl and stir the parsley into it, then divide the broth among four ramekins; chill the ramekins until the broth has set — about two hours.

Slice the beef and arrange it with the vegetables on individual lettuce-lined plates. Briefly dip the bottom of a ramekin into hot water; invert the ramekin onto one of the plates to release the jellied broth, then lift away the mold. Unmold the other ramekins in the same way. Serve the salads with the mayonnaise alongside.

Beef and Apple Salad with Stilton Cheese Dressing

Serves 4 as a main course
Working time: about 40 minutes
Total time: about 1 hour and 20 minutes

Calories **340**
Protein **28g.**
Cholesterol **91mg.**
Total fat **16g.**
Saturated fat **6g.**
Sodium **515mg.**

14 oz. beef round roast
1 tbsp. cracked black peppercorns
½ cup stout or dark beer
¼ cup grated fresh horseradish, or 2 tbsp. prepared horseradish, drained
½ cup finely chopped shallot
1 cup chopped celery
2 tart green apples, peeled, cored and cut into small pieces
2 tbsp. cut fresh chives
1 bunch of watercress, washed and dried
3½ tbsp. mayonnaise (recipe, page 13)
2 oz. Stilton cheese, crumbled
juice of 1 lemon
¼ tsp. salt

Preheat the oven to 450° F. Rub the beef with the cracked pepper, pressing the grains into the roast with the palm of your hand. Heat a heavy-bottomed oven-proof skillet over medium-high heat. Set the beef in the skillet with its fat side down; briefly sear the beef to render some of the fat. When a thin layer of fat covers the bottom of the skillet, turn the beef over and brown it on the other side. Continue turning the beef until it is browned all over — about five minutes.

Transfer the skillet to the oven and roast the beef for 10 minutes. Remove the skillet and pour ¼ cup of the stout or beer over the roast. Return the roast to the oven and cook it until it is medium rare — about 20 minutes more. Remove the roast from the skillet and set it aside to cool.

Pour the remaining ¼ cup of stout or beer into the skillet and set it over medium-high heat. Simmer the liquid, scraping the bottom of the skillet with a wooden spoon until any caramelized juices have dissolved — about two minutes. Pour the liquid into a small heatproof bowl; set the bowl in the freezer for about 30 minutes.

While the liquid is chilling, assemble the rest of the salad. Trim the roast of fat and cut the beef into julienne. Transfer the beef to a large bowl and add the horseradish, shallot, celery, apples and chives. Pluck the leaves from half of the watercress stems and add the leaves to the mixture.

To make the dressing, lift the layer of congealed fat from the surface of the chilled liquid. Whisk the liquid with the mayonnaise, cheese, lemon juice and salt. Pour the dressing over the contents of the bowl and toss the salad well. Present the salad on a serving platter, garnished with the remaining watercress.

4 Microwaved scallops and zucchini nestle in a wreath of shredded radicchio (recipe, page 129). The salad is dressed with a ginger vinaigrette.

Surprising Paths to Freshness

Unexpected refinements in the salad maker's art can be achieved with a microwave oven. The microwave allows a multitude of salad ingredients to be prepared with a fine touch, be they vegetables, seafood or fowl. And whether the intended effect is simple or sophisticated, the preparation and assembly of a salad are accomplished in short order: For the nine recipes that follow, the working time averages just a little more than 20 minutes.

Chief among the microwave's qualifications for salad making is the gentle treatment it accords all manner of fresh vegetables, from the asparagus for molded timbales on page 136 to the zucchini, mushrooms and red pepper that compose the Vegetable Salad à la Grecque on page 133. Thanks to their abbreviated cooking time and the little water needed to cook them, these vegetables emerge from the oven with their nutrients, texture and brilliant color intact. By the same token, traditionally slow-cooking root vegetables may be quickly readied to form the base of a salad: In the recipes in this section, beets are done in just six to eight minutes, potatoes in 12 to 14.

Even the mainstays of fish and shellfish salads can be handled — with care — in the microwave. In Salade Niçoise *(page 130)*, thinly sliced fresh tuna is poached for several minutes in a dressing of tarragon, Dijon mustard and stock taken piping hot from the microwave oven; the tuna is then tossed with other elements of the salad and chilled before serving. Scallops, too, are ideally suited for the microwave process; to the benefit of the chilled main-course salad in which they are highlighted *(page 129)*, the scallops retain their full measure of moisture and flavor.

Not to be overlooked is the microwave's versatility when it comes to preparing salad dressings. In some cases, the microwave produces a dressing that is poured over the salad while the liquid is still hot. The potato salad on page 132, for example, features a hot dressing based on celery, red onion and bacon, while the key to creating the wilted-spinach salad on page 135 is a hot dressing of rice vinegar, sugar, soy sauce and pearl onions.

Because power settings often vary among different manufacturers' ovens, the recipes use ''high'' to indicate 100 percent power, ''medium high'' for 70 percent and ''medium low'' for 30 percent.

Scallop and Zucchini Salad on a Bed of Radicchio

Serves 4 as a main course at lunch
Working time: about 15 minutes
Total time: about 40 minutes

Calories **120**
Protein **15g.**
Cholesterol **31mg.**
Total fat **4g.**
Saturated fat **1g.**
Sodium **210mg.**

¾ lb. sea scallops, rinsed, the bright white connective tissue removed
1 small zucchini (about ¼ lb.), trimmed and cut into paper-thin slices
2 tbsp. thinly sliced crystallized ginger
2½ tbsp. fresh lemon juice
¼ tsp. salt
freshly ground black pepper
1 tbsp. virgin olive oil
1 head of radicchio or red-leaf lettuce (about ¼ lb.), washed, dried and cut into chiffonade (technique, page 51)

Slice the scallops into very thin rounds. In a shallow glass bowl, combine the scallops with the zucchini, 1½ tablespoons of the ginger, 1½ tablespoons of the lemon juice, the salt and some pepper. Set the bowl aside for five minutes; stir the contents and allow them to stand for five minutes more.

Microwave the scallops and zucchini in their marinade for two to three minutes on high, stirring midway through the cooking.

Put the remaining ½ tablespoon of ginger in a small bowl. Set a strainer over the bowl and pour the scallop mixture into the strainer. Refrigerate both strainer and bowl for at least 15 minutes.

At the end of the chilling time, whisk the remaining tablespoon of lemon juice, the oil and some more pepper into the marinade; then stir in the scallop mixture. Arrange the chiffonade in the shape of a wreath on a plate. Mound the salad in the center and serve at once.

Salade Niçoise

Serves 4 as a main course
Working time: about 30 minutes
Total time: about 1 hour and 45 minutes
(includes chilling)

Calories **380**
Protein **35g.**
Cholesterol **44mg.**
Total fat **13g.**
Saturated fat **2g.**
Sodium **210mg.**

1 lb. small round red potatoes
½ lb. green beans, trimmed
3 oil-cured black olives, pitted and coarsely chopped
½ lb. ripe plum tomatoes, cored and cut into ½-inch-thick slices
2 hard-boiled eggs, the yolks discarded, the whites coarsely chopped
2 tbsp. white wine vinegar
2 tbsp. chopped fresh tarragon, or 2 tsp. dried tarragon
2 tsp. Dijon mustard
1 small red onion, peeled, sliced and separated into rings
1 garlic clove, finely chopped
6 tbsp. fish stock or unsalted chicken stock
freshly ground black pepper
1 lb. fresh tuna fillet, cut into ½-inch-wide strips
1 tbsp. virgin olive oil
3 heads of Bibb lettuce, washed and dried

Prick the potatoes with a fork in two places; any more punctures would let too much moisture escape. Arrange them in a circle in the microwave oven and cook them on high for four minutes. Turn the potatoes over and rearrange them in the oven; continue cooking them until they are barely tender — three to four minutes more. Set them aside to cool.

While the potatoes are cooling, cook the beans: Put them in a bowl and pour in ¼ cup of water. Cover the bowl with a lid or plastic wrap and microwave on high until the beans are tender but still crisp — three to four minutes. Drain the beans and refresh them under cold running water, then drain them again and transfer them to a salad bowl. Peel the potatoes and cut them into 1-inch chunks. Add the potatoes, olives, tomatoes and egg whites to the beans.

Dry the bowl in which you cooked the beans and combine the vinegar, tarragon, mustard, onion, garlic, stock and some pepper in it. Cook the mixture on high until it reaches a boil — about three minutes. Remove the bowl from the oven. Rinse the tuna, pat it dry, and add it to the bowl. Stir the contents to distribute the tuna, then cover the bowl tightly, and set it aside for three minutes. The tuna should be opaque and firm to the touch; if it is not, drain the liquid into another bowl, reheat it, and pour it over the tuna strips for a second three-minute steeping.

Add the cooked tuna and its steeping liquid to the bowl containing the beans. Pour in the oil and toss the ingredients gently. Refrigerate the salad for at least 45 minutes before serving it on a bed of lettuce leaves.

Julienned Beets with Dijon Mustard

Serves 4 as a first course
Working time: about 15 minutes
Total time: about 30 minutes

Calories **70**
Protein **1g.**
Cholesterol **0mg.**
Total fat **4g.**
Saturated fat **0g.**
Sodium **115mg.**

3 medium beets of equal size (about ¾ lb.)
1 shallot, finely chopped
1½ tbsp. Dijon mustard
1½ tbsp. red wine vinegar
freshly ground black pepper
1 tbsp. virgin olive oil
1 small head of Boston lettuce or 1 head of Bibb lettuce (about ¼ lb.), washed and dried

Rinse the beets but do not pat them dry. Put the beets on a plate and microwave them on high for six to eight minutes, turning them over about halfway through the cooking time. Remove the beets from the oven, wrap them in a single large piece of aluminum foil, and let them stand for 15 minutes to complete their cooking.

In a small bowl, combine the shallot, mustard, vinegar, some pepper and 1 tablespoon of water. Whisk in the oil and set the vinaigrette aside.

Peel and julienne the beets. Combine the julienne with about three fourths of the vinaigrette; toss the beets well and refrigerate them until they are cool.

Just before serving time, slice the lettuce into chiffonade *(technique, page 51)* and toss it with the remaining vinaigrette. Divide the lettuce evenly among four salad plates, top with the beets, and serve at once.

Bacon and Onion Potato Salad

Serves 6 as a side dish
Working time: about 10 minutes
Total time: about 20 minutes

Calories **140**
Protein **3g.**
Cholesterol **2mg.**
Total fat **2g.**
Saturated fat **0g.**
Sodium **45mg.**

2 lb. small round red potatoes of equal size, scrubbed
2 strips bacon, cut into thin pieces
⅓ cup thinly sliced red onion
¼ cup finely chopped celery
1 tbsp. cornstarch, mixed with ½ cup unsalted chicken stock
¼ cup white vinegar
freshly ground black pepper
2 tbsp. coarsely chopped fresh parsley

Prick the potatoes with a fork in two places; any more punctures would let too much moisture escape. Arrange them in a circle in the microwave oven; cook them on high for seven minutes. Turn the potatoes over and rearrange them; continue cooking them on high until they are barely soft — five to seven minutes more. Remove the potatoes from the oven and set them aside until they are cool enough to handle.

Put the bacon strips in a bowl; cover the bowl with a paper towel and microwave the bacon on high for two minutes. Remove the towel and drain off the excess fat, then add the onion and celery to the bowl. Toss the bacon and vegetables together, cover the bowl with plastic wrap, and microwave on high for 90 seconds. Stir in the cornstarch mixture along with the vinegar. Cover the bowl and microwave it on high until the dressing thickens slightly — about two minutes.

Cut the potatoes into slices about ¼ inch thick. Pour the dressing over the potato slices; sprinkle in a generous grinding of pepper and 1 tablespoon of the parsley. Gently toss the salad, then allow it to cool somewhat. Scatter the remaining parsley over the top just before serving the dish.

Vegetable Salad à la Grecque

Serves 8 as a side dish
Working time: about 35 minutes
Total time: about 1 hour

Calories **45**
Protein **2g.**
Cholesterol **0mg.**
Total fat **2g.**
Saturated fat **0g.**
Sodium **70mg.**

1 leek, trimmed, split, washed thoroughly to remove all grit, and thinly sliced
4 garlic cloves, sliced
2 zucchini (about 1 lb.), cut into 1-inch-long cylinders and quartered lengthwise
½ lb. mushrooms, wiped clean and sliced
juice of 1 lemon
1 sweet red pepper, seeded, deribbed and cut lengthwise into thin strips
1 tsp. chopped fresh thyme, or ¼ tsp. dried thyme leaves
½ tsp. chopped fresh rosemary, or ¼ tsp. dried rosemary, crumbled
¼ tsp. fennel seeds, crushed
¼ tsp. salt
freshly ground black pepper
1 tbsp. virgin olive oil

Place the leek and garlic in a shallow baking dish. Pour in ½ cup of water and cover the dish with heavy-duty plastic wrap. Microwave the dish on high for four minutes, stirring the vegetables after two minutes. With a slotted spoon, transfer the leeks and garlic to a large bowl, leaving as much liquid as possible in the dish.

Put the zucchini into the dish, cover it again with plastic wrap and microwave it on high for three minutes. Using the slotted spoon, transfer the zucchini to the bowl containing the leeks.

Place the mushrooms in the dish and pour in the lemon juice; cover once more and cook the mixture on high for two minutes. Again using the slotted spoon, transfer the mushrooms to the bowl containing the leek-and-zucchini mixture.

Next, stir the pepper strips into the liquid, cover the dish, and cook the pepper strips on high for two minutes. Use the slotted spoon to transfer the red pepper to the bowl containing the other vegetables.

Stir the thyme, rosemary and fennel seeds into the liquid remaining in the dish. Cook the liquid, uncovered, on high for eight minutes, stirring it every two minutes. Pour the hot liquid over the vegetables in the bowl, then sprinkle the salt and some pepper over the vegetables. Let the salad marinate until it cools to room temperature — about 30 minutes.

Just before serving, pour the oil over the vegetables and toss the salad well.

Duck and Wild Rice Salad with Raspberry Vinaigrette

Serves 6 as a main course at lunch
Working time: about 30 minutes
Total time: about 3 hours and 10 minutes
(includes chilling)

Calories **310**	
Protein **25g.**	
Cholesterol **76mg.**	
Total fat **12g.**	
Saturated fat **4g.**	
Sodium **110mg.**	

one 4-lb. duck, rinsed and patted dry	1 tbsp. finely chopped shallot
5 tbsp. raspberry vinegar	freshly ground black pepper
1 cup wild rice	3 tbsp. unsalted chicken stock or water
1 garlic clove, finely chopped	2 tsp. safflower oil
1 cup julienned carrot	1 small head of red-leaf lettuce, washed and dried
1 cup julienned celery	1 small head of escarole, washed and dried
1 large ripe tomato, peeled, seeded and coarsely chopped	
1 tsp. Dijon mustard	

Trim any excess fat from around the neck of the duck. Remove any fat from the cavity. To release body fat from the duck without rendering its juices as it cooks, lightly prick the duck, taking care not to pierce the flesh below the layer of fat. Using wooden picks, fasten the neck skin to the back of the duck. Sprinkle the inside of the cavity with 1 tablespoon of the vinegar. Place the duck breast side down in a microwave-safe roasting pan and cover it with wax paper. Microwave the duck on medium high (70 percent power) for 15 minutes. Drain off and discard the fat in the roasting pan. Turn the duck breast side up and cover it with fresh wax paper. Continue cooking the duck on medium high until the juices run clear when a thigh is pierced with the tip of a sharp knife — about 20 minutes. Drain off and discard the fat, and set the duck aside to cool.

Meanwhile, bring 2½ cups of water to a boil in a saucepan. Pour the water into a bowl and add the wild rice and garlic. Cover the bowl and microwave the rice on medium low (30 percent power) until it is tender — about 30 minutes. Drain the rice, transfer it to a large bowl, and refrigerate it.

Put the carrot and celery julienne into a bowl with 2 tablespoons of hot water. Cover the bowl and microwave the vegetables on high until they are tender — two to three minutes. Drain the vegetables and combine them with the rice; return the mixture to the refrigerator.

When the duck is cool enough to handle, pull off its skin. Cut the meat from the duck and slice it into thin strips. Toss the strips with the rice-and-vegetable mixture. Stir in the tomato and 2 tablespoons of the remaining vinegar, and set the bowl aside.

In a small bowl, combine the mustard, shallot, some pepper, the remaining 2 tablespoons of vinegar and the stock or water. Whisking vigorously, pour in the oil in a thin, steady stream; continue whisking until the mixture is well combined. Pour the vinaigrette over the duck mixture and toss it well. Chill the salad for about two hours to meld its flavors.

To serve the salad, arrange the lettuce and escarole leaves on a serving platter and mound the salad on top of them. Serve immediately.

Wilted Spinach Salad

Serves 4 as a side dish
Working time: about 15 minutes
Total time: about 20 minutes

Calories **95**
Protein **5g.**
Cholesterol **0mg**
Total fat **1g.**
Saturated fat **0g.**
Sodium **200mg.**

⅓ cup rice vinegar

1 tbsp. sugar

2 tsp. low-sodium soy sauce

2 tsp. sweet chili sauce

2 tbsp. cornstarch, mixed with ½ cup unsalted chicken stock

½ lb. canned straw mushrooms, drained, the stem tips cut off, or 10 oz. fresh mushrooms, wiped clean and stemmed

1 cup pearl onions, blanched in boiling water for 2 minutes and peeled

1 lb. fresh spinach, washed, stemmed, dried and torn into pieces

1 sheet nori, crumbled (optional)

Combine all of the ingredients but the spinach and nori in a bowl. Stir the mixture well, then microwave it on high until it thickens slightly — about three minutes. Thoroughly stir the dressing again, then pour it over the spinach. Toss the spinach to coat it evenly; sprinkle it with the nori if you are using it, and serve the salad at once.

Barley Salad with Orange-Shallot Dressing

Serves 10 as a side dish
Working time: about 25 minutes
Total time: about 1 hour and 15 minutes

Calories **125**
Protein **4g.**
Cholesterol **5mg.**
Total fat **4g.**
Saturated fat **1g.**
Sodium **85mg.**

1 cup pearl barley
4 shallots, finely chopped
1 garlic clove, finely chopped
1 orange, the juice reserved, the zest grated
2 oz. Canadian bacon cut into ¼-inch cubes
¼ cup chopped fresh parsley
2 tbsp. safflower oil
4 ripe plum tomatoes, sliced

Bring 4 cups of water to a boil and pour it into a 4-quart bowl. Add the barley, cover the bowl and microwave the barley on high, stirring it every five minutes, until it is tender — about 25 minutes. Let the barley stand for at least 10 minutes.

To prepare the dressing, combine the shallots, garlic, orange juice, ½ teaspoon of the grated zest and the bacon in a shallow dish. Cover the dish and microwave the dressing on high for two minutes.

Drain the barley and stir in the dressing. Let the salad stand until it cools to room temperature — about 30 minutes. Mix the parsley and oil into the salad, garnish it with the tomato slices, and serve at once.

Molded Asparagus Timbales

Serves 6 as a first course
Working time: about 30 minutes
Total time: about 6 hours and 30 minutes
(includes chilling)

Calories **60**
Protein **7g.**
Cholesterol **2mg.**
Total fat **2g.**
Saturated fat **1g.**
Sodium **110mg.**

1 lb. medium asparagus, trimmed and peeled
1 cup cold unsalted chicken stock
1 tsp. unflavored powdered gelatin
¼ lb. firm tofu
½ cup low-fat (preferably 1 percent) cottage cheese
½ cup plain low-fat yogurt
2 scallions, trimmed and coarsely chopped
1 jalapeño pepper, seeded (caution, page 17)
3 tbsp. finely cut fresh dill, or 1 tbsp. dried dill mixed with 2 tbsp. chopped fresh parsley
lettuce leaves, washed and dried, for garnish

Arrange the asparagus stalks in a single layer on a dinner plate. Cover the plate tightly with heavy-duty plastic wrap and microwave the asparagus on high for two to three minutes, rotating the plate a quarter turn midway through the cooking. Set the asparagus stalks aside but do not uncover them.

Pour the stock into a 2-cup glass measuring cup. Sprinkle the gelatin over the stock and stir it in. Microwave the mixture on high for four minutes, then stir it to ensure that the gelatin has dissolved. If it has not, microwave the mixture for one minute more.

Purée the tofu, cottage cheese, yogurt, scallions, jalapeño pepper, and dill or dill-and-parsley mixture in a food processor or blender. Pour the purée into a large bowl and stir in the gelatin mixture. Set the bowl aside.

Cut off and reserve 18 asparagus tips for garnish. Coarsely chop the remaining asparagus and combine it with the gelatin mixture. Divide the mixture evenly among six ½-cup ramekins. Refrigerate the ramekins until the mixture has set — at least six hours.

To serve, run the tip of a knife around the inside of a ramekin to loosen the sides of the timbale. Set the ramekin in a shallow bowl of hot water for 15 seconds to loosen the bottom, then invert the timbale onto a small plate. Repeat the process to unmold the other timbales. Garnish each with three asparagus tips; arrange a few lettuce leaves around the timbale and serve immediately.

TARRAGON

THYME

BASIL

A Wreath of Salad Herbs

The 14 herbs depicted here are all called for in this book. Fresh are generally preferred over the dried, both for flavor and color, but dried herbs may be substituted in most instances and thus the recipes list dried as options wherever appropriate.

Increasingly, herbs are arriving in the markets fresh; the proliferation of farmers' markets across the country has widened choice. And many cooks with gardens have taken to raising their own. Recent ethnic influences have called attention to once seemingly esoteric herbs. Cilantro, for one, is at last gaining deserved popularity in the United States, although Asians, Latins and Moroccans, among others, have been using it for centuries.

Anyone wishing to dry fresh herbs can tie them loosely in a bundle and hang them upside down in a cool, dark, well-ventilated place for several weeks. When the leaves are completely dried, strip them from the stems and store them in an airtight container.

Two swifter methods of preserving herbs make use of the microwave oven and the freezer. To microwave herbs, place five or six sprigs at a time between paper towels and microwave them on high for one to three minutes until the leaves are brittle. Store the leaves loosely in airtight jars.

To freeze herbs, rinse the sprigs and pat them dry. Strip the leaves off the stems and put them into a heavy-duty plastic bag. Gently flatten the bag to force out the air, seal the bag tightly, and place it in your freezer. Use the leaves as the need arises.

Basil (also called sweet basil): This fragrant herb, with its underlying flavor of anise and hint of clove, goes particularly well with tomato.

Chervil: The small, lacy leaves of this herb have a taste akin to parsley with a touch of anise. It is good in salads and salad dressings. Chervil is popular in France where it is often an ingredient in herb mixtures, including *fines herbes*. When used in cooking, chervil should be added at the end, lest its subtle flavor be lost.

Chives: The smallest of the onions, chives grow in grassy clumps. When finely cut, the hollow leaves contribute their delicate, oniony flavor to fresh salads and raw vegetables. Chives should always be used fresh, as dried ones are virtually tasteless.

Cilantro (also called Chinese parsley): The serrated leaves of the coriander plant impart a distinctive fragrance and a flavor that is both mildly sweet and bitter. Cilantro leaves should be used fresh or added at the end of cooking if their flavor is to be appreciated fully.

Dill: A sprightly herb with feathery leaves, dill enhances cucumber and many other fresh vegetables, as well as fish and shellfish. When used in cooking, dill should be added toward the end of the process to preserve its delicate flavor. Both dill seeds and

CHERVIL

CILANTRO

CHIVES

ROSEMARY

SAGE

PARSLEY, FLAT

139

PARSLEY, CURLY

OREGANO

dill leaves can be steeped for several weeks in a bottle of white, cider or white wine vinegar to make an herbed vinegar.

Marjoram (also called sweet marjoram): A native of the Mediterranean, this perfumed herb has tender, small green leaves. The flavor is similar to that of oregano, only more subtle. Whole leaves may be used to flavor salads; they can also be added fresh or dried to salad dressings.

Mint: Of this large family of herbs, the most common variety is spearmint, depicted here. Spearmint leaves, with their serrated edges and pebbly surfaces, have a sweeter taste than peppermint. They contribute a refreshing sparkle to salads; spearmint sprigs make attractive garnishes.

Oregano: This robust, strong-smelling herb with a trace of bitterness lends character to salads and salad dressings. A close relative of marjoram, oregano has leaves that are generally larger and more pointed. The flavor of the leaves intensifies when oregano is dried.

Parsley, curly: The most common fresh herb on the market, clean-tasting curly parsley is widely used to garnish salads but has enough character in its own right to be an integral part of many salad preparations.

Parsley, flat (also called Italian parsley): A relative of the popular curly parsley, it has straight, broad leaves that many cooks prefer for their flavor, more distinct than that of curly parsley.

Rosemary: A rich-smelling herb, with an almost piney aroma, this native of the Mediterranean grows as a shrubby evergreen. Like oregano, sage and thyme, rosemary retains much of its flavor after drying and stays potent through cooking. It is often paired with roasted and grilled meats, especially lamb.

Sage: The resin-scented, grayish green leaves have a hint of bitterness and of camphor. Chopped, they may be added to salads, poultry stuffings and pork. Dried, they not only retain much of their flavor, but a pleasant muskiness emerges.

Tarragon: A delightful anise flavor permeates the leaves of this herb. The French variety is preferred. A tarragon-flavored vinegar can readily be made by steeping whole sprigs of the herb in a bottle of vinegar for several weeks; the sprigs may be left in the bottle.

Thyme: The tiny leaves of this herb pack an abundance of earthy flavor. Thyme can be added fresh or dried to salads, salad dressings and vinegars. It is an essential component in a *bouquet garni,* along with parsley and bay leaf. Thyme leaves dry well.

MARJORAM

DILL

MINT

Glossary

Al dente: an Italian term meaning "to the tooth." It is used to describe the texture and taste of perfectly cooked pasta: chewy but with no flavor of flour.

Almond oil: a highly fragrant oil used in small amounts to flavor salads. Its traditional role is as a flavoring agent in confectionery.

Ancho chili pepper: a mild, dark reddish brown dried poblano chili pepper.

Arugula: see page 8.

Balsamic vinegar: a mildly acidic, intensely fragrant wine-based vinegar made in Modena, Italy; traditionally it is aged in wooden casks.

Basil: see page 138.

Bâtonnet: French for "little stick." Used to describe the size and shape of vegetables cut into pieces about 1½ inches long and ¼ inch square.

Belgian endive: see page 8.

Black vinegar, Chinese (also called Chenkong vinegar and Chinkiang vinegar): a dark vinegar made from fermented rice.

Blanch: to partially cook food by immersing it briefly in boiling water.

Bulgur: whole-wheat kernels that have been steamed, dried and cracked.

Calimyrna figs: a variety of green fig grown in California.

Calorie (or kilocalorie): a unit of heat measurement, used to gauge the amount of energy a food supplies when it is broken down for use in the body.

Capers: the pickled flower buds of the caper plant, a shrub native to the Mediterranean. Capers should be rinsed before use to rid them of excess salt.

Cardamom: the bittersweet, aromatic dried seed pods of a plant in the ginger family. Cardamom seeds may be used whole or ground.

Celeriac (also called celery root): the knobby, tuberous root of a plant in the celery family.

Cepes (also called porcini): wild mushrooms with a pungent, earthy flavor that survives drying or long cooking. Dried cepes should be soaked in water before they are used.

Chayote (also called mirliton): a pear-shaped, pale-green squash that retains its crispness when cooked.

Chervil: see page 138

Chicory: see Curly endive, page 8

Chili paste: a robust, spicy paste made of chili peppers, salt and various other ingredients. Numerous kinds are available in Asian markets.

Chili pepper: any of several varieties of red or green pepper with an extremely hot taste. Whether fresh or dried, chili peppers contain volatile oils that can irritate the skin and eyes; they must be handled with the utmost care *(caution, page 17)*.

Chinese black vinegar: see Black vinegar, Chinese.

Chinese cabbage: see Nappa cabbage, page 10.

Chinese long beans: a variety of green bean that averages a foot in length. Chinese long beans are more tender than standard green beans; they are available in Asian produce markets.

Chinese parsley: see Cilantro, page 138.

Chives: see page 138.

Cholesterol: a waxlike substance that is manufactured in the human liver and is also found in foods of animal origin. Although a certain amount of cholesterol is necessary for producing hormones and building cell walls, an excess can accumulate in the arteries, contributing to heart disease. See also Monounsaturated fat; Polyunsaturated fat; Saturated fat.

Cilantro: see page 131.

Coriander: an herb whose earthy-tasting seeds are a basic ingredient in curries. The leaves go under the name cilantro.

Corn salad: see Mâche, page 9.

Couscous: a fine-grained semolina pasta, traditionally served as a base for the classic North African stew of the same name.

Crenshaw melon: a gold and green melon, with shallow lengthwise surface grooves and salmon-colored, rich-tasting flesh.

Crystallized ginger (also called candied ginger): stems of ginger preserved with sugar. Crystallized ginger should not be confused with ginger in syrup.

Cubanelle pepper: a brightly colored mild pepper with thick, sweet flesh.

Cumin: the seeds of a plant related to caraway. Crushed cumin seeds lend a pleasantly bitter flavor to curry powder and chili powder; when toasted, they have a nutty taste.

Curly endive: see page 8.

Daikon radish: a long, white Japanese radish.

Dandelion greens: see page 9.

Dark sesame oil: a dark seasoning oil, high in polyunsaturated fats, that is made from toasted sesame seeds. Because dark sesame oil has a relatively low smoking point, it is rarely heated. Dark sesame oil should not be confused or replaced with lighter sesame cooking oils.

Debeard: to remove the fibrous threads from a mussel. These threads, called the beard, are produced by the mussel to attach itself to stationary objects.

Devein: to remove the intestinal vein that runs along the outer curve of a shrimp. To devein a shrimp, peel it first, then make a shallow cut along the line of the vein and scrape out the vein with the tip of the knife.

Dijon mustard: a smooth mustard once manufactured only in Dijon, France; it may be flavored with herbs, green peppercorns or white wine.

Dill: see page 138.

Ditalini: a short, dried tubular pasta.

Escarole: see page 9.

Farfalline: a dried pasta shaped like little bow ties.

Fat: a basic component of many foods, containing three types of fatty acids — saturated, monounsaturated and polyunsaturated — in varying proportions. See also Monounsaturated fat; Polyunsaturated fat; Saturated fat.

Fava beans (also called broad beans): a European variety of bean, eaten fresh or dried. The thick pods and thin skins must be removed from all but the youngest fava beans.

Fennel (also called anise, finocchio and Florence fennel): a vegetable with feathery green tops and a thick, white, bulbous stalk. It has a milky, licorice flavor and can be eaten raw or cooked.

Fermented black beans: soybeans that have been fermented, dried and salted. Fermented black beans should be rinsed before use to rid them of excess salt.

Five-spice powder: a pungent blend of ground Sichuan pepper, star anise, cassia, cloves and fennel seeds; available in Asian groceries.

Ginger: the spicy, buff-colored rhizome, or rootlike stem, of the ginger plant, used as a seasoning either in fresh form or dried and powdered. Dried ginger makes a poor substitute for fresh. See also Crystallized ginger.

Hoisin sauce: a thick, dark reddish brown sauce customarily made from soybeans, flour, garlic, sugar and spices.

Hot red-pepper sauce: a hot, unsweetened chili sauce such as Tabasco®.

Jalapeño chili pepper: a squat, green, hot chili pepper, essential to a number of Mexican dishes. See also Chili pepper.

Jerusalem artichoke (also called sunchoke): neither from Jerusalem nor an artichoke, this American vegetable is the tuberous root of a member of the sunflower family. In texture, color and flavor, it resembles the water chestnut.

Jícama: a globular root vegetable with brown skin, ranging in weight from one to four pounds. Its white flesh stays crunchy even after cooking.

Julienne: to slice a food into matchstick-size pieces.

Kale: see page 9.

Kasha: toasted buckwheat groats.

Kohlrabi: a vegetable with an enlarged stem in the form of a light-green or lavender bulb.

Lamb's lettuce: see Mâche, page 9.

Mâche: see page 9.

Marjoram: see page 139.

Millet: a nutritious grain with a nutty, mild taste.

Mint: see page 139.

Mirin: a sweetened Japanese cooking wine made from rice. If mirin is unavailable, substitute white wine or sake mixed with a little sugar.

Monkfish (also called angler, bellyfish and goosefish): an Atlantic fish with lean, firm, somewhat dry flesh. Its flavor reminds some of lobster.

Monounsaturated fat: one of the three types of fatty acids found in fats. Monounsaturated fats are believed not to raise the level of cholesterol in the blood. Some oils high in monounsaturated fats — olive oil, for example — are thought to lower the blood-cholesterol level.

Mustard greens: see page 10.

Nappa cabbage: see page 10.

Nonreactive pan: a cooking vessel whose surface does not react chemically with the acids in food. Ovenproof clay, stainless steel, enamel, glass and nonstick-coated aluminum are all considered nonreactive materials.

Nori: paper-like dark green or black sheets of dried seaweed, often used in Japanese cuisine as a flavoring agent or as wrappers for rice and vegetables.

Oakleaf lettuce: see page 10.

Olive oil: any of various grades of oil extracted from olives. Extra virgin olive oil has a full, fruity flavor and very low acidity. Virgin olive oil is lighter in flavor and slightly higher in acidity. Pure olive oil, a processed blend of olive oils, has the lightest taste and the highest acidity. For salad dressings, virgin and extra virgin olive oils are preferred.

Orange roughy: a fish caught off the coast of New Zealand and available, usually as frozen fillets, all year round. Its firm, white flesh breaks into large flakes when it is cooked.

Orzo: a rice-shaped dried pasta.

Pancetta: a salted — not smoked — Italian bacon, available at Italian delicatessens.

Parsley: see page 139.

Penne: a tubular dried pasta with diagonally cut ends. The word is Italian for "pens" or "quills."

Pine nuts: (also called pignoli): seeds from the cone of the stone pine, a tree native to the Mediterranean. The buttery flavor of pine nuts can be heightened by light toasting.

Polenta: cooked cornmeal, traditionally eaten in Northern Italy.

Polyunsaturated fat: one of the three types of fatty acids found in fats. It exists in abundance in such vegetable oils as safflower, corn and soybean. Polyunsaturated fats lower the level of cholesterol in the blood.

Prosciutto: an air-cured ham that is sliced paper-thin. The best is produced near Parma, Italy.

Radicchio: see page 11.

Recommended Dietary Allowance (RDA): the average required daily amount of an essential nutrient as determined for groups of healthy people of various ages by the National Research Council.

Red chicory: see Radicchio, page 11.

Reduce: to boil down a liquid in order to concentrate its flavor and thicken its consistency.

Refresh: to rinse a briefly cooked vegetable under cold water to arrest its cooking and set its color.

Rice vinegar: a mild, fragrant vinegar that is less assertive than cider vinegar or distilled white vinegar. It is available in dark, light, seasoned and sweetened varieties; Japanese rice vinegar generally is milder than the Chinese version.

Rocket: see Arugula, page 8.

Rosemary: see page 139.

Rotini: a spiral-shaped dried pasta.

Safflower oil: the vegetable oil that contains the highest proportion of polyunsaturated fats.

Saffron: the dried, yellowish red stigmas (or threads) of the flower of *Crocus sativus;* saffron yields a pungent flavor and a brilliant yellow color.

Sage: see page 139.

Saturated fat: one of the three types of fatty acids present in fats. Found in abundance in animal products and in coconut and palm oils, saturated fats raise the level of blood cholesterol. Because high blood-cholesterol levels contribute to heart disease, saturated-fat consumption should be kept to a minimum — preferably less than 10 percent of the calories consumed each day.

Savoy cabbage: see page 11.

Sesame oil: see Dark sesame oil.

Sesame paste (also called tahini): a nutty-tasting paste made from ground sesame seeds.

Seviche (ceviche): originally, a Peruvian dish made of raw white fish or scallops combined with lemon or lime juice, onion, hot red-pepper flakes and black peppercorns. The term is now often used for any dish in which fish or shellfish marinates in citrus juice.

Sherry vinegar: a full-bodied vinegar made from sherry; its distinguishing feature is a sweet aftertaste.

Shiitake mushrooms: a variety of mushroom, originally grown only in Japan, sold fresh or dried. The dried form should be soaked and stemmed before use.

Sichuan pepper (also called anise pepper, Chinese pepper and Japanese pepper): the dried berry of a shrub native to China. Its flavor is tart and aromatic, but less piquant than that of black pepper.

Snow peas: small, flat green pea pods, eaten whole with only the stems and strings removed.

Sodium: a nutrient essential to maintaining the proper balance of fluids in the body. In most diets, a major source of the element is table salt, made up of 40 percent sodium. Excess sodium may contribute to high blood pressure, which increases the risk of heart disease. One teaspoon of salt — with about 2,100 milligrams of sodium — contains almost two thirds of the maximum "safe and adequate" daily intake recommended by the National Research Council.

Sorrel: see page 11.

Soy sauce: a savory, salty brown liquid made from fermented soybeans. One tablespoon of regular soy sauce contains about 1,030 milligrams of sodium; lower-sodium variations may contain as little as half that amount.

Stock: a savory liquid, most often used as a flavor-rich base for sauces, that is made by simmering aromatic vegetables, herbs, spices, bones and meat trimmings in water. Unsalted, defatted chicken or veal stock is often used to enrich the dressings in this book without adding unwanted fat.

Straw mushrooms: cultivated mushrooms with pointed caps and a silky texture. Straw mushrooms are usually available in either cans or jars.

Sugar snap peas: a variation of garden pea introduced in 1979; when stem and string are removed, the entire pod may be eaten.

Sun-dried tomatoes: tomatoes that have been dried in the open air to concentrate their flavor; some are then packed in oil. Most sun-dried tomatoes are of Italian origin, but they are now being produced in the United States, too.

Tarragon: see page 139.

Thyme: see page 139.

Tofu (also called bean curd): a dense, custard-like soybean product with a mild flavor. Tofu is rich in protein, relatively low in calories and free of cholesterol. It is highly perishable and should be kept refrigerated, submerged in water; if the water is changed daily, the tofu may be stored for up to a week.

Tomatillo: a small, tart, green, tomato-like fruit vegetable that is covered with a loose, papery husk. It is frequently used in Mexican dishes.

Total fat: an individual's daily intake of polyunsaturated, monounsaturated and saturated fats. Nutritionists recommend that fat constitute no more than 30 percent of a person's total calorie intake. The term as used in the nutrient analyses in this book refers to all the sources of fat in a recipe.

Virgin olive oil: see Olive oil.

Walnut oil: an oil extracted from pressed walnuts. Its distinctive flavor adds balance to such bitter greens as curly endive. It should be purchased in small quantities; once opened, it can turn rancid within just a few weeks.

Water chestnuts: the walnut-size tubers of an aquatic Asian plant, with rough brown skin and white, sweet, crisp flesh. Fresh water chestnuts may be refrigerated for up to two weeks; they must be peeled before use.

Watercress: see page 11.

Wheat berries: unpolished, whole-wheat kernels with a nutty taste and chewy texture.

Wild rice: the seeds of a water grass native to the Great Lakes region of the United States. Wild rice is appreciated for its robust flavor.

Zest: the flavorful outermost layer of citrus-fruit rind, cut or grated free of the bitter white pith that lies beneath it.

Ziti: dried tubular pasta about 1½ inches long.

Index

Picture Credits

All photographs in this book were taken by staff photographer Renée Comet unless otherwise indicated: Cover: Steven Biver. 2: top and center, Carolyn Wall Rothery. 5: left, Steven Biver; right, Michael Latil. 8-11: Michael Latil. 16, 17: Taran Z. 34: Michael Latil. 37: Taran Z. 40: Michael Geiger. 43: top, Taran Z. 44: bottom, Michael Latil. 45: Michael Latil. 47: top, Michael Latil. 50: Taran Z. 51: left, Taran Z. 55: Taran Z. 57: top, Michael Latil. 59: Michael Latil. 60: Taran Z. 62: Michael Latil. 63: Taran Z. 66: Michael Latil. 67: Steven Biver. 68-70: Michael Latil. 72: Taran Z. 73: Steven Biver. 77: Michael Latil. 78, 79: Steven Biver. 81: Michael Latil. 82: Steven Biver. 85, 86: Michael Latil. 88: Michael Latil. 90: Michael Latil. 91: Steven Biver. 93: Michael Latil. 96: Michael Ward. 99: Michael Ward. 105, 106: Steven Biver. 109: Steven Biver. 110: top, Michael Ward. 112: Steven Biver. 113: right, Michael Ward. 114: Michael Geiger. 115: Michael Latil. 117: bottom, Michael Latil. 118: Michael Latil. 120: Steven Biver. 121: Michael Latil. 124: Michael Latil. 125: Steven Biver. 130: Michael Ward. 132: Michael Ward. 133: Michael Latil. 134-136: Michael Ward. 137: Michael Latil. 138, 139: Taran Z.

Props: cover: plates, Ann Mallory, A. Mallory California, Santa Barbara, Calif.; placemat, Dorothy Turk, Clay J Tabletop Accessories, Santa Barbara, Calif. 18: Susquehanna Antique Co., Inc., Washington, D.C. 21: Margaret Donnald, Enamelists Gallery, Torpedo Factory Art Center, Alexandria, Va. 23: Ellen Godwin. 24: Exotica Wood Works, Appalachian Spring, Washington, D.C. 26: Donna Polseno, The American Hand Plus, Washington, D.C. 27: plate, Orsini (Gwen An-

derson), Enamelists Gallery, Torpedo Factory Art Center; fan, Jean Thompson, Torpedo Factory Art Center. 28: Paula Steele's Country Antiques & Folk Art, Bowie, Md. 29: Royal Worcester Spode Inc., New York. 30: Mariposa, New York. 31: platter, Nambé Mills Inc., Santa Fe, N. Mex.; juicer, T. R. Benton. 32: top, Richard Meier for Swid Powell, The American Hand Plus. 33: ramekins, Charles F. Lamalle, New York; plate, Elayne De Vito. 35: The Mediterranean Shop, New York. 36: Country Lace Antiques, Bowie, Md. 38: Micheline's Country French Antiques, Alexandria, Va. 40: small bowl, Full Circle, Alexandria, Va.; spoon, La Cuisine, Alexandria, Va. 42: Stanley Andersen, The American Hand Plus. 43: Ellen Godwin. 45: Hutschenreuther Corporation, New York. 51: Susie Cohen, Alexandria, Va. 52: The Pineapple Country Collection, Alexandria, Va. 54: Tim Mather, The American Hand Plus. 55: Jinny De Paul, Going to Pot, Torpedo Factory Art Center. 56: Anne Carr's Old Town Antiques, Alexandria, Va.; fabric, Country Lace Antiques. 58: mold, The Iron Gate Antiques, Inc., Washington, D.C. 60: Thaxton & Co., New York. 61: Mariposa. 62: Deborah Geiger by Harriet Anderson, Enamelists Gallery, Torpedo Factory Art Center. 63: Brendan & Backer Antiques, Washington, D.C. 64-65: jars, Betty Carr, Pleasant Walk Antiques and Herb Farm, Myersville, Md.; metal surface, Melvin Comet. 67: Preferred Stock, Washington, D.C. 68: Fil Caravan Inc., New York. 69: Zona, New York. 70: Martin's of Georgetown, Washington, D.C. 71: Page/Thorbeck Studio, Seattle, Wash. 73: Preferred Stock. 74: Mabel's Kountry Store, Alexandria, Va. 75: Ann Morhauser, Santa Cruz, Calif. 78: Fredrick B. Hanson Country Antiques, Keedysville, Md. 80: Vietri Inc.,

Chapel Hill, N.C. 81: Evergreen Antiques, New York. 82: Jean Cohen, Full Circle. 83: Tom Phinney, Oberlin, Ohio. 84: Marc Westen Decorative Arts, Washington, D.C.; fabric, Joyce Piotrowski. 85: Mary George Kronstadt, Jackie Chalkley Fine Crafts and Wearables, Washington, D.C. 86: Brendan & Backer Antiques. 87: David Bennett. 88: Preferred Stock. 89: Judith Salomon, The American Hand Plus. 91: Mieko and Michael Kahn, Appalachiana, Bethesda, Md. 92: Gertrude Berman. 94-95: Mariposa. 96: Marston Luce Antiques, Washington D.C. 97: The Pilgrim Glass Corp., New York. 98: The Flower Designer, Washington, D.C. 99: Lynn A. Ascher. 100: Marston Luce Antiques. 101: Margaret Chatelain, Bristol, Vt. 102: Judith K. Zieve, Helen Drutt Gallery, Philadelphia, Pa. 103: Bill Schwaneflugel, One Step Up, Bethesda, Md. 104: David Nelson, The American Hand Plus. 105: Reynolds & Wilhoit Antiques, Washington, D.C. 106: Preferred Stock. 107: Priscilla Manning Porter, Appalachiana. 109: Brendan & Backer Antiques. 110: left, Ann Morhauser. 113: right, Sherry Schuster, The Warm Glass Studio, Lakewood, N.J. 115: Antiques by Ann Brinkley, Washington, D.C. 116: plates, Marc Westen Decorative Arts; spice tins, Mabel's Kountry Store. 117: top, Annieglass, Santa Cruz, Calif. 118: Franco Antiques, Washington, D.C. 119: Scandinavian Galleries, Washington, D.C. 120: Judith K. Zieve, Helen Drutt Gallery. 122: Franco Antiques. 123: Silverman Galleries, Alexandria, Va. 126: Constance Talbot, High Hollow Pottery, Windsor, Mass. 128: Sandra Selesnick, Full Circle. 131: Marston Luce Antiques. 132: Marc Westen Decorative Arts. 133: Silverman Galleries. 135: Uzzolo, Washington, D.C. 137: Melvin and Stella Cohen.

Acknowledgments

The index for this book was prepared by Dick Mudrow. The editors are particularly indebted to the following people for creating recipes for this volume: Leslie Bloom, Silver Spring, Md.; Nora Carey, Paris; Carole Clements, Paris; Sharon Farrington, Bethesda, Md.; Michael Krondl, New York; Shahnaz Mehta, McLean, Va.; Tina Ujlaki, New York.

The editors also wish to thank: Jo Calabrese, Royal Worcester Spode Inc., New York; Jackie Chalkley, Fine Crafts and Wearables, Washington, D.C.; Nic Colling, Home Produce Company, Alexandria, Va.; Margaret Berry Cotton, Hanover, N.H.; Jeanne Dale, The Pilgrim Glass Corp., New York; Rex Downey, Oxon Hill, Md.; Flowers Unique, Alexandria, Va.;

Flying Foods, International, Long Island City, N.Y.; Dennis Garrett, Ed Nash, The American Hand Plus, Washington, D.C.; Giant Foods, Inc., Landover, Md.; Judith Goodkind, Alexandria, Va.; Chong Su Han, Grass Roots Restaurant, Alexandria, Va.; Ken Hancock, Annandale, Va.; Joe Huffer, Mount Solon, Va.; Imperial Produce, Washington, D.C.; Kitchen Bazaar, Washington, D.C.; Kossow Gourmet Produce, Washington, D.C.; Gary Latzman, Kirk Phillips, Retroneu, New York; Magruder's, Inc., Rockville, Md.; Sara Mark, Alexandria, Va.; Nambé Mills Inc., Santa Fe, New Mexico; Andrew Naylor, Alexandria, Va.; Hiu Newcomb, Potomac Vegetable Farms, Vienna, Va.; Lisa Ownby, Alexandria, Va.; Joyce Piotrowski, Vienna, Va.; RT's Restaurant, Alexandria, Va.; Ann Ready,

Alexandria, Va.; Linda Robertson, JUD Tile, Vienna, Va.; Safeway Stores, Inc., Landover, Md.; Bert Saunders, WILTON Armetale, New York; Nancy Snyder, Snyder's Sprouts, Rockville, Md.; Straight from the Crate, Inc.; Alexandria, Va.; Sutton Place Gourmet, Washington, D.C.; Kathy Swekel, Columbia, Md.; Nancy Teksten, National Onion Association, Greeley, Colorado; 219 Restaurant, Alexandria, Va.; U.S. Fish, Kensington, Md.; Williams-Sonoma, Washington, D.C.; Lynn Addison Yorke, Cheverly, Md.
The editors wish to thank the following for their donation of kitchen equipment: Le Creuset, distributed by Schiller & Asmus, Inc., Yemasse, S.C.; Cuisinarts, Inc., Greenwich, Conn.; KitchenAid, Inc., Troy, Ohio; Oster, Milwaukee, Wis.

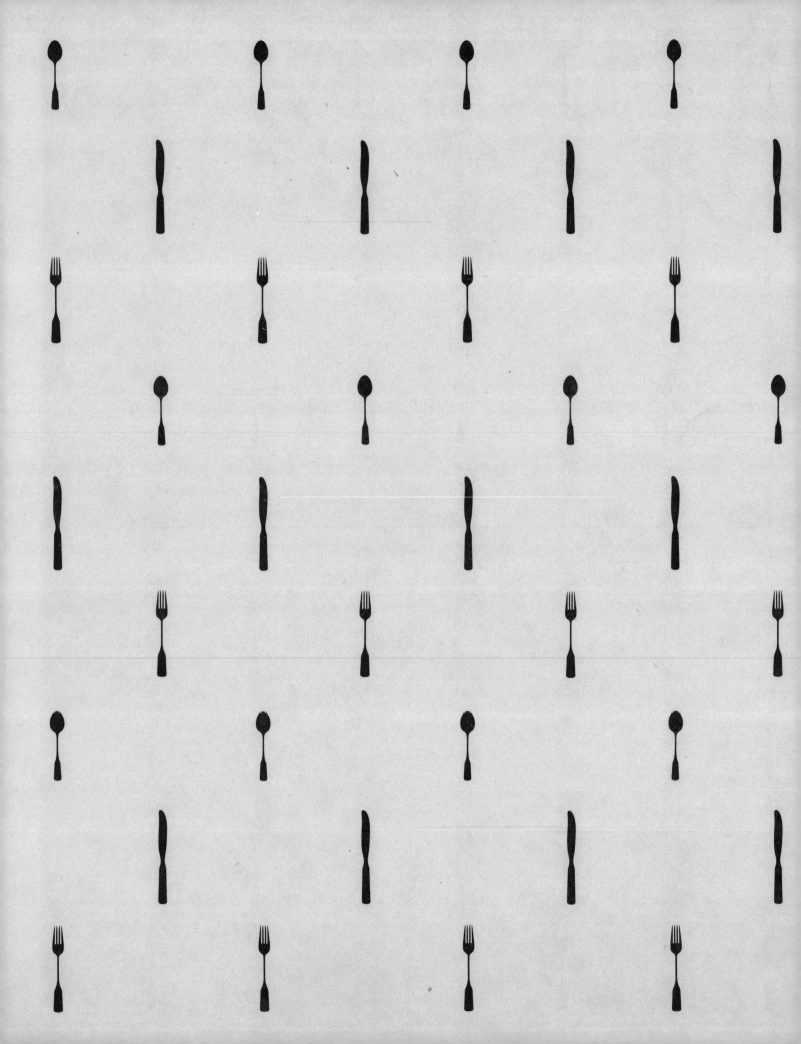